D0919552

THAT THE MEDALS
AND THE
BATON BE PUT ON VIEW

THAT THE MEDALS
AND THE
BATON BE PUT ON VIEW

The story of a Village Band
1875–1975

Henry Livings

DAVID & CHARLES
Newton Abbot London
North Pomfret (VT) Vancouver

Some of the photographs here are from our family albums, newspaper cuttings and ancient records, so we hope you will forgive any lack of clarity and definition.

ISBN 0 7153 7071 5
Library of Congress Catalog Card Number 75–10721

Set in 11 on 13pt Baskerville
and printed in Great Britain
by Biddles Ltd Guildford
for David & Charles (Holdings) Limited
South Devon House   Newton Abbot   Devon

Published in the United States of America
by David & Charles Inc
North Pomfret   Vermont 05053   USA

Published in Canada
by Douglas David & Charles Limited
132 Philip Avenue   North Vancouver   BC

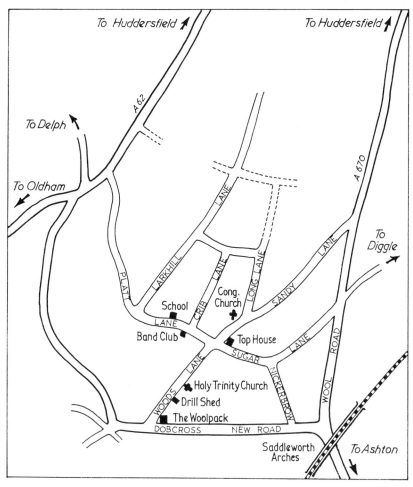

The village of Dobcross

Stand on the massive gritstone slabs of Dinnerstones, with the valley of the Colne River behind you, and below and before you the first springs and streams of the Tame, which is a tributary of the Mersey. The ancient glacier scoured out two shallow valleys, and between them is the green whale-hump of Harrop Edge, curving down Lark Hill at the far end; and there is Dobcross, in the Parish of Saddleworth.

The crossroads which forms the village square linked the whole valley of Saddleworth with the woollen mills and markets of Oldham and Huddersfield, Wakefield and Manchester, Hull and Liverpool; the Saddleworth woolmasters had offices in New York; and from this crossroads the Saddleworth Bank issued its notes, at *The Swan Inn* overlooking the square the magistrates sat.

Since Ashton took our water (to sell back to us) and the Huddersfield/Ashton canal was built, the valley bottoms became less marshy, the turnpikes could be built there and pass either side of us, and bedamned to them.

There's some Victorian infilling, some Accrington brick ribbon

Dobcross in the early 1900s

development from the sad thirties, two council estates, and two 'executive-type' commuter estates, but the core of the village was built in the age of George II, the richest age in literature, architecture, art and military savagery since Queen Elizabeth. And a very handsome place it is, with tall stone-built, stone-slated houses, mostly three-storey, rows of stone-mullioned windows (a yard by half a yard) for the weavers to catch every bit of daylight going, each dwelling jammed against the next, for company and for shelter against the wild weather.

Now the weaving is done in the big mills, and there's a dyeworks, cornmill, industrial tubing works, three metalworks, a meter manufactory, besides smaller businesses and the farms (beef, dairy, pigs, sheep and a mouse-farm)—all this, and yet the River Tame is clean, the trout loiter, and the ducks breed like ducks.

And the noblest sight of the year, on Whit Friday morning, is the Dobcross Band. In scarlet and black, Nelson Peters in his drummer's apron, a knife-edge crease to his trousers and his uniform cap at a rakish angle over a face that a medieval craftsman

Dobcross today

Dobcross marching to the wedding of their trombonist, David Ibbotson

would have carved in oak, detonates the big drum, and twenty-five players, plus snare drum, set off with 'Hail Smiling Morn' to join and lead the village procession and the Church and Congregational banners.

George Gibson, conductor, leads the band, a big man in every way, with the swift light movements bulky men sometimes have, a rosy face with baby-blue eyes that can catch you out with a sly wit, and a vast paunch; marching, as he puts it, 'in a smart and air-manlike manner', which somehow manages to convey a gleeful complicity at the same time. Better perhaps to leave this scene for the moment, until its significance has been filled out some.

First, a quick guide to the instruments, taking them in order of size: ten cornets. The cornet is a three-valved conical bore instrument, softer and more melodious than the trumpet, but similar in range and appearance. There are ten in a formal brass band, starting with the soprano, which has the highest pitch of any instrument in the band, and I sometimes wonder how come the player's knees don't rise up to his chin in certain pieces.

The rest of the cornets are slightly bigger and identical; there's the solo cornet–the 'leader' in orchestral terms, and three first cornets, the tutti, less elegantly known as bumpers-up. Then there's two each of the second and third cornets, for the texture and power; often scored for rythmic accompaniment to the firsts, the after-beats ('umchucks' to the vulgar). There's also a position of some importance occupied by the repiano cornet, which, together with the flugelhorn, can play the under-melody. The flugelhorn looks like a bigger cornet, and though it may share the same copy as the rep, is basically a solo instrument, with its own musical figures to make.

Next in ascending order of size, the three tenor horns: these you hold with the bell pointing up, and they link into the lower range of the flugel, with low notes at the upper end of the French horn's register.

Next the baritone horns, two of them; composers frequently neglect the virtuoso possibilities of this instrument (and murder the player with work in the ensemble), which can range from the cornet's register right down to the bass's. It's one of the hardest to play well, and rewards a good player with a fine, strong sound.

Next, the euphonium, the most melodious of brass band instruments. Often takes the French horn part in works adapted from orchestral scores, unjustly in my opinion, as it hasn't the rasp and force that the baritone has naturally. Marcus Cutts, the distinguished euphonium player from the Fairey Band, plays tuba occasionally with the Hallé, which is correct, as the other name for the euph is the tenor tuba. There's really almost no limit to the capacities of a great player: I heard Marcus one time play a solo piece which belonged rightly to the bassoon, and if you closed your eyes, you *heard* the distinctive tone of the woodwind. Next the trombones, first, second, and that magniloquent voice of the underworld, the bass trombone. I think it's safe to say that the most successful composers for brass band are the ones who respect the versatility of the trombone, which can give grandeur to a note which would merely be raucous on another instrument and then surprise you with a tender melody.

Finally, the E flat and the double B flat bombardons, known to us as the basses. The ground and foundation of the brass band sound: two of each, and a good bass section makes the floor tremble. All the instruments are usually silvered to keep them bright, but they're brass all right. This complement of twenty-five players, plus conductor ('who may not play' as they say in the contest rules) and percussion nowadays, has become conventional because of the need to have regular contest rules; there's nothing magical about it, and quartets, quintets, and octets sound fine; mind, this is not an argument likely to be accepted by a concert secretary who's booked you for a full band.

The clear, bright brassy sound used in orchestral works, and in dance band music, is not much sought in brass banding, where vibrato, properly controlled is accepted and expected; in the context of fiddles violas etc, it would be foolish of a trumpet player to expect to distinguish himself by the softness of his tone, and useless on a dance-floor; whereas of course, in the brass band, brass is offering the full range of tone. John Ireland called them 'silver orchestras', which was friendly of him, but they're imitation nothing. A Victorian writer described the great Besses' o' th' Barn Band as having the 'sound of a mighty organ', which is fair, as instrument to instrument there is a blend, a homogeneity of sound; but it's also very flexible, it can give you contrasts of wit, vulgar hilarity, as well as schmaltz, oompah, deep nobility and fastidious musical balance. Most of all it needs to be *seen:* you need to see the cornets and trombones raised in fanfare, the lonely liquid soprano against the massed tapestry of the ensemble, the basses hoisted for their thunder. And moster than that, you need the privilege of knowing the bandsmen, of supporting your own band, because it's a social thing–if only for practical reasons: a set of instruments can cost over £5,000, and even a decent cornet is around the £100 mark.

The back-up organisation is formidable, with a band management committee and a ladies' committee (usually concerned with raising money for a particular objective such as uniforms, instruments, perhaps pelmets for the music stands); in our case there is the club committee, the vice-presidents (local worthies), the librarian, the band sergeant . . . you have to get together, to have a band at all.

So, the history of the Dobcross Band. There was a band here which collapsed in or before 1875; I can say this because in that year the treasurer of the Congregational church notes a repayment of £5 'from the late Dobcross Amateur Brass Band'. I seem to feel the faint chill of a secretary unable to turn out a full band for some rashly accepted booking, the seething and accusatory resentment of disappointed churchmen, the hotfoot search for musicians to make up the numbers, the reckless promises of fees to entice them. I also suspect they had unhelpful competition. We have a book of minutes, which begins 15 September 1875, and in it there's a poignant page recording practices in April and May, 1876:

Sunday April 16
In the Banks near Mr. Eastwoods reservoir
The Band had a practice.
April 23rd. Sunday, Band practice Platt Lane
(April) 30 Sunday Band practice. Ladcastle End.
Only played one piece ... day bitter cold ... snow fell.
Adjourned into Band room, played two pieces ...
[14 May]: Sunday forenoon, Short Band practice, Platt Lane
the rain which stopped them.

Whatever the 'Band room' was, it wasn't a home, and they seem reluctant to practice there; I imagine no one takes pleasure in making his mistakes en plein air, but they were going to have a blow choosehow.

The men who made up that old band, and who managed its affairs, may not have been ambitious in the ordinary sense, but they considered that they mattered, and in the end they were proved right. This was the village and this the band that was to build its own club, draw the best of players to it, produce and train championship players for bands throughout the brass band movement,

The first entry in the minute book

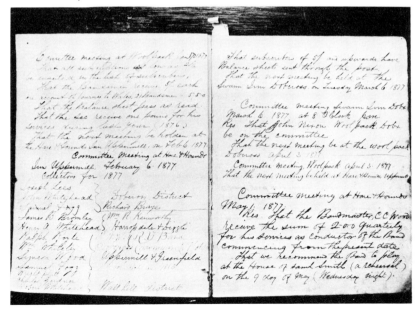

and finally, to win the Championship of Champions.

By 5 August 1876, they were fit to take third prize at Oldham Contest (under the name of the 34th West Yorkshire Rifle Volunteer Band) and on 24 August 1876, they were at 'the Welch contest at Rhaddyher in Montgomeryshire' to win a first prize of £50 ... well worth picking up today, and a heady moment at any point in a band's history.

In 1877, John Haigh, Secretary, is recording the annual election of the committee, and arrangements for collecting subscriptions, even in neighbouring villages.

Diggle and Greenfield both had their own bands, the collectors must have gone by night; the same goes for Delph (and Denshaw and Royal George, all within the boundaries of Saddleworth), but I think they circumspectly left Delph out on account of the fierce and warlike natives. Pitched battles took place in the streets of Greenfield, Diggle and Delph for lesser causes.

The committee met in different inns; twenty committeemen were elected, including officers, and John Nixon, landlord of *The Woolpack Inn* in Dobcross, was later co-opted; seven was the quorum, but it was seldom met, and the committee still had to function, so by the end of the year, five was voted a sufficient quorum.

No innkeeper would turn away drinking men, and being host to the committee would also mean that he'd be caught for a subscription, and would have a personal visit from the band when they 'played round for the gentlemen'. If he gave more than 5s he'd get a balance sheet through the post, and so he ought, it was real money: a foundryman was taking seventy hours to earn £1 3s 4d, and the bandmaster, C. C. Wood, a distinguished local musician who also conducted a string band just over Lark Hill in the valley of Castleshaw, had £8 for his year's services 1877-88.

The Band, bereft of organisation and a home, had inserted itself into the establishment of the local Rifle Volunteers, the 34th West Yorkshire. They thus acquired both a uniform and a hall for practice. The drill shed, with parallel dwellings for officers and NCOs, still stands in Woods Lane.

On Saturday 20 October 1877, at three o'clock, John Nixon fetched a meal from *The Woolpack* (just down the lane) for sixty-five people. After they'd eaten, there was a ball: Gentlemen 6d, Ladies

A Rifle Volunteer

12

The Woods Lane drill hall; officers' quarters nearest

4d. 'N.B.,' writes John Haigh, 'This will be the 3rd. annual dinner in connection with the 34 W.Y.R.V. Band.' For the academics among us, and assuming you have to be in existence a year before you have your first annual dinner, that should mean that the band started its continuous existence in 1873 at the earliest, 1875 at the latest. The 'Dobcross Amateur Brass Band' fades like the Cheshire Cat, and the smile is rueful.

The English tend to think of themselves an an unmilitary race; the French, with their unseemly love of glory, had introduced conscription in 1872, the Japanese, morbidly fascinated by death in the field, conscripted from 1873. The English, on the other hand, lovers both of personal liberty and low taxation, had it both ways with an enthusiastic Rifle Volunteer militia, and the (mounted) Yeomanry. These were the troops who helped turn the tide against the Boers later, and it was the Yeomanry that sabred the Chartists at Peterloo in Manchester. Shaw Boden, who lived in one of the dwellings connected with the drill shed at the end of his life, told me of marching out as a child from the Platt Lane Primary School under the discipline of the drill sergeant in the nineties. Mind you, the unit was disbanded in disgrace after they'd booed the CO at a parade in Huddersfield. This man had driven the sergeant to suicide, and seems to have been something of a martinet: certain it is he wasn't from Saddleworth. One can guess at the mental torment of the sergeant, bred in the area, with a countryman's steady and patient ways, where organisation is more by osmosis than by edict and command, where your neighbour's fathers were your father's neighbours, confronted by a harsh and vigilant commander. The connection with the Rifle Volunteers lasted until 1883, when an acrimonius minute was recorded at *The Swan Inn, Dobcross, 23 August.*

At a General Meeting Held at the Swan Inn, August 23, 1883, the following motions were made and past

1st That the Royal George band have stifelio at the sum of one pound without trial

2nd That the band to hereby agree to Serve In the Corps for 2 Years for the sum of £60-0-0 together with the Rifle Cloths—on a respectable engagement

3rd That if the Corps will not accept the above turns, we will give up the services altogether

4th That the Band agrees to go to the D&D CC proffessionals Benefit on the 1st of Sept

5th That Sam Littlewood takes the symbols and tries to endeavour to amend himself

Rifle Volunteers could be fined by the Magistrates for not attending parades, and the mind blanks out at the notion of hoping that bandsmen would accept that kind of discipline. There's a saga running through the minute book at this time, which starts 6 June 1883, when it's decided 'That Alfred Hirst be suspended for misconduct ... arrange return instruments etc ... and pay all damage ... and arrears due'. Three years later we find the entry: 'That Alfred Hirst pays 25s for the instrument that has been repaired'. The saga continues 15 June 1887: 'That the Flugelhorn that has been repaired be brought before the Band to see whether the Bandsmen or the Committee settle the matter, as the player wishes to leave'.

Communal pressure having proved useless, they succeeded by bureaucracy: 2 July 1888: 'that Alfred Hirst has half his coming engagement remuneration deducted till he has paid for the Flugelhorn'.

There are as many different ways of paying and not paying bandsmen as there are bands; in our band it's traditional for them to share money collected playing Christmas carols, and the fee for playing in the Whit Friday processions. Nothing else. At the other end of the scale there are firms who pay retainers, and a member of a colliery band was overheard asking where the pithead was, he didn't want to bump into it by mistake.

However, in spite of tensions, they were progressive times while the War Office was supporting the band, and they the Rifle Volunteers. C.C. Wood's pay as bandmaster was upped for 1878-9 to £13, on condition that he took three practices a week (with a deduction of 1s 8d for non-attendance). The secretary got £1 for his services, and if my experience is anything to go by, it cost him a lot more than that to have the job.

Three new instruments were ordered from Bessons 'viz. E Flat soprano cornet, flugle horn and flugle horn B flat ... the flugle horn B flat not electro plated'. Note, two flugelhorns, where the band now features only one. The band minutes refer on several occasions to revisions of band rules, and make application to other bands for theirs so that they can compare them with their own. These may have been articles of association, laying down democratic processes and purposes (how many committeemen, how elected, how long for etc) but they are evidence of a feeling of belonging to a general movement, and of wishing to conform to accepted standards and practices. They must also have had to consider the instrumental composition of the band, if only so that they could make the same amount of noise as other bands at contests. Without the professionals' yardsticks of critical and financial success, contests are as good a way as any of measuring your musical progress ... and of course contest successes bring more concert bookings. Judges are chosen (we piously hope) for their musical distinction, and judge the bands unseen, each in its class, from 'Championship' down to the humble Fourth Class band. The concept of the 'test-piece'–bands in each class having to play the same composition–can make for boring listening if you're not counting points for your favourite, with band after band squeezing the last dram of savour out of the music, and bands can fall into the trap of training for the one event like muscle-bound athletes. The notion of a 'test-piece' seems to have gained ascendancy following the Norland Contest in 1887, and Joseph N. Hampson, early historian of the Besses' o' th' Barn Band rails vigorously for several pages against 'the exulting craze'. 'Own-choice' contests are certainly more fun.

Anyway, instrumental composition was still far from fixed. A band contest took place as early as 1821, when bands taking part in processions in the Manchester area to celebrate the coronation of George IV held an ad hoc competition to while away the time as the procession was being marshalled. The early contests must have been exuberant occasions, with insane musical monuments to English, French and German invention, like the serpent (a vast curling woodwind, as you might imagine an alpenhorn left out in the sun; there is a brass version), the keyed bugle, the ophecleide (brass bassoon: *why?*) and brass clarinet, with cornets, horns, trombones and bombardon.

In 1859, Loftus Band Contest called for 'fourteen players, professionals barred'. In 1892, Besses won Belle Vue (and incidentally every other major challenge cup in Great Britain) with twenty-four players: a soprano, seven cornets, two flugelhorns, three tenor horns, two baritones, two euphoniums, two tenor and one G trombone, two E flat bombardons, one medium bass B flat, and a monstre basso. I should like to see that last one: I can't imagine a man walking about with anything bigger than a double B.

Our band was figuring modestly in contests 1877-8: third (£12) at Oldham, second (£15) at Staleybridge, second at Mossley, and £7 and a cornet at Northenden Contest.

The band anniversary was celebrated 23 November 1878, 4 pm at the drill shed with a tea-party for 150 people. There was 'reciting, solos, duetts, Glees, Madrigals', and music by the band, of various sorts, also music for dancing at intervals. Beef and ham to £2 0s 4d was made up into sandwiches, requiring 8lb of butter; liquor 1s 4d. The profit was £4 16s 7d.

And in 1884, a new E flat bombardon was bought from Bessons (£11); John Radcliffe was getting £21 per year as conductor.

This sort of money was raised by concerts, subscriptions (from the public, bandsmen themselves do not seem at this time to have had to pay for the privilege of playing), a fee from the Rifle Volunteers, and draws. On 29 June 1887, John Schofield ('Jack Warper' pronounced 'Waaper' ... if you asked for John Schofield in Saddleworth, twenty men would reply), secretary, is instructed to write to the Delph and Dobcross Cricket Club secretary 'to inform him that we cannot put our draw off as we have got all in preparation.

2nd. That the tickets be passed as read.' It wasn't until August, two months later, that bandsmen went round the district soliciting prizes, but they weren't having those cricketers telling them when they could or couldn't have their draw.

It's interesting to note that in spite of a massive boom in textiles between 1884 and 1888, there's no reference in the minute book to suggest any direct support from industrialists. Smoke billowed out of the mill chimneys so that any morning you could write your name in the soot on your windows, trees were blighted at fifteen foot, and streams and river were poisoned.

The Dobcross patent four-by-four-box loom, the first important commercial automatic loom on which colour-changes could be made while the machine was running, was manufactured at Diggle Foundry, and they were exporting 1,000 of them every year.

Yet the immediate and more well-heeled supporters of the band were H. A. Whitehead (baker) and John Nixon (landlord of *The Woolpack*); Lieut-Col Taylor is the most distinguished name mentioned at this time, good for a donation of £1. The Mallalieus, the Kenworthys, the Bradburys and the Tanners, big mill-owners living in the valley, as they mostly still do, were perhaps canvassed personally, but never as firms; and if that did happen, there's no sign of it in the minutes.

I think it was to be borne in mind that a good proportion of the working people could still get by on their own handlooms, weaving blankets, shawls or linsey (coarse woollen dress material, made of shoddy); if they couldn't, they certainly remembered their parents doing it as a regular thing. Piecework rates, arrived at by bargain-

Wharmton Wood as it was in about 1900. The trees had a burnt appearance owing to the huge amounts of acid in the air

ing, were and are normal. When the weavers of Bankfield Mill struck in 1896, they came out against low wages, but also spoke of 'the present inferiority of the material as being the greatest drawback in this dispute. Also we want to stop the introduction of two price lists in this district, namely: men and women'.

If you do not treat as equals, in short, we don't treat.

The music was, until just before World War I, and with the exception of marches, mostly derivative: 'Gems from Beethoven', 'Selection from the Gondoliers', 'Salute to Sullivan', but the sound was and is entirely original. As the goatherd's pipe, the mother's lullaby or the herald's fanfare are natural products of a useful activity, so is the sound of a brass band.

Our lives may be sliced in two by the need for wages, may be artificially split into labour and leisure in a way that a farmer or a mother hardly understands; but we heal the cut when we make music, because we belong to a place, to lead our processions, to advertise a firm, to celebrate our seasons.

The relationship with the 34th West Yorkshire Rifle Volunteers was not an easy one for these reasons. The unquestioned and unquestioning authority of even a part-time soldier doesn't fit with the self-respect and independent commitment of banding. Even in April 1878 the committee was considering 'taking the upper room at the top of Dobcross' (presumably an unused second-floor originally used for handloom weaving); and in January 1886, when the 'respectable engagement' of 1883 ran out, there are signs of a band in full flounder:

Committee Meeting Held at the Kings Head Inn Dobcross.
Resolved 1st That the Contribution be two Pence Per Week.
2nd That we give 1-6 per week for Band Room at Tamewater rates all cleared.
3rd That all spare Instruments be Brought in to I. M. Treasurer.
Chairman Robert Whitehead.

Tamewater is away from the centre of the village, and the band weren't there long. They settled finally, and for twenty years, in a room (about 16ft x 12ft) up a flight of stone steps on the opposite side of the lane to the drill shed. It was built on to *The Nudger Inn* (*The Hark to Nudger*, named after a trail hound), with *The Hark to Bounty Hark* (they knew how to name a dog in those days) on the other side.

The band room and *The Nudger* are now demolished, to make way for 'superior' dwellings, the fabulous bowling green neglected and gone. When I knew the band room it was far gone in disrepair, and had a noisome gents underneath which I was often glad to see, and no doubt the bandsmen were too: they soon developed a system whereby they let down a jug on a rope for ale from *The Nudger*, and, according to legend, suffered embarrassment when the Constable came across the dangling jug at some unacceptable hour. This may account for a rule promulgated 9 February 1898: 'That all intoxicating beverages must not be brought on any consideration on Sunday. Anybody wanting it must bring in on Saturdays'.

The minutes from 1886 to 1892 make dismal reading, as the committee wheedle and manoeuvre, cajole and command, to get the bandsmen together and to sustain the finances. Anybody who has ever served on a committee (and what Englishman hasn't?) will know and understand the desolation of working for a cause which is in disarray. A request was made to the Dobcross Dramatic Society to see if 'they could give them a Drama performance for the benefit of the Band. At their earliest opportunity'. There's no evidence that any benefit came of it. John Roberts got £5 towards his salary as

The *Nudger* band room

conductor on 8 January 1888, 'the remainder to be paid as soon as possible'. On Saturday, 9 February 1889, the band played in the Square 'as a tendency for subscriptions'. They even sent Booth Roberts, John B. Kenworthy, and Charles Kenworthy to collect in Delph.

The pictures show them in their maturity, sixteen years later: in 1889 they were reckless and desperate men.

John Schofield's copperplate records the sadness of it all.

There was total failure to get a meeting at all from February to October, no great loss either, the state things were in. Three attempts were made in August: on 13 Aug, 'the following motion was made and pass that this meeting be postponed until Saturday night August 17th'. Saturday, 17 August came and went unrecorded, and on 25 Aug is the entry 'not a majority of the Committee appeared, so the Meeting was postponed'.

Now a good and vigorous committee is not necessarily the mark of a good band: your conductor could be a world-famous maestro, your band be playing superbly, your bandmaster a revered and powerful father to the band, your band sergeant firm and wise, the secretary, treasurer and librarian may be overwhelmed by an avalanche of bookings and the funds rolling in, and the committee

Booth Roberts

be an enfeebled bunch of dunderheads; all I can say is, I've never seen it like that.

Suddenly, in 1892, the tone of the minutes changes completely. John Schofield continues as secretary, steady and true, and the whole organisation is tightened up. No more minutes about tea--pourers and begging the Congregational church to put on a benefit for the band. We're buying instruments, and telegraphing for them, deputing men to go and collect them from Rochdale and have '15s between', getting new players. The bandmaster, Booth Roberts, is chairman, and he means business.

Bands are democratic, and they respect and support a man of stature if his example and leadership go in a direction they can accept.

This may be as good a time as any to outline the hierarchy. Treasurer and Secretary explain themselves I hope; the one you make efforts to trust, the other you burden with labours an indentured coolie would reject. Librarian, well, he catalogues and preserves the scores, distributes and collects them. Band Sergeant marshalls the band ('Come on lads, sup up'), carries out the Bandmaster's instructions ('Dickie bows, no caps') and may have to sack a player or move him to a different instrument ('The committee has

Left Charles Kenworthy   Minutes of January 1889

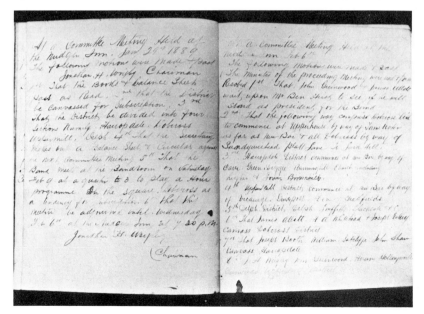

March 1892 Kings Head Delions

1st Motion. That I write to Edward sykes
Causeway set. Nr Delph. for is terms.

2nd That I write to Richard Beade to bring
is Instruments in and Uniform Inn. at once

3rd That Wike Turner has 2nd Trombone.

4th That Hulect Howautt has Soprano

5th That Joseph Shaw is asked to have a cornet

6th That I write to Wm Booth to see if the
Instruments are ready.

7th That WH Byrom & R Whitehead fetch the
instruments Back from Wm Booth

8th The next meeting will be on Friday
next the 26 inst. all members noticed

Chairman Booth Roberts

Minutes of March 1892

decided …'). The Bandmaster is the cohesive power, the executive, and moves by consensus and custom. If he's dictatorial or weak, and doesn't command the respect of the band, they just go–no excuses, no explanations–there's just suddenly no band. And the basses hang neglected, while the committee finds itself making hollow noises '… that so-and-so bring in his instrument and uniform forthwith. Which was complied with'. If the band is in funds and ambitious, they'll employ a conductor, or musical director, whose business will be entirely musical … and championship bands now bring in men of musical distinction to polish their performances for important occasions. In leaner times, the bandmaster is also the conductor.

Incidentally, if a band folds, it's almost impossible to know what to do with the instruments. There's a set which belonged to the Denshaw Band in this valley, which may never be played again. Trustees are appointed, but the instruments will have been bought by public subscription, so whose are they but the property of ghosts?

Ted Sykes held the job of conductor with us, at 2s 6d a practice, until 1894, when James Henry Buckley came onto the scene. A neighbour described him as 'a smart man, with a lot to say for himself', and the evidence is he was a character of some dimension. Members of his family still live in the village, and they carry his mark: wilful and intelligent, careless of the opinions of others. I'm a Buckley myself on my mother's side, and certainly I have the dark hair, grey eyes and curved nose … I could use some of the vigour. The band committee didn't really know what to do with J. H. Buckley: he was paid, retrospectively, 30s for 1895. This was nothing like the money that, for instance, C. C. Wood had had sixteen years previously, and no doubt he knew it. The cost of living was stable, but it wasn't going down. The committee settled on £3 for the coming year. Two days later they'd had some conversation with him which prompted '… and should the Band be in a good financial position at the end of the year, they will make him a present'. There's no record of him getting the present.

The committee, be it noted, were talking about three practices a week for this £3 per annum; in 1898 Horatio Bamforth took home 34s 6d for a forty-eight hour week at the foundry, so Mr Buckley wasn't asking for the Crown Jewels. Mind, they knew their man, and we don't, but I think I get his flavour.

By 1898, things were getting huffy; meeting followed meeting.

Meeting Held January 7th 1898.

No I That we do not pay the Conductor 8£ a year

No II That we make him an offer of 5£ for the year 1898 for his Services as Conductor.

No III That the Secretary write to the Conductor with regard to the offer of 5£.

No IV That the Secretary be supplied with 2 new Books.

No V That no money be paid without the sanction of the committee to the offices.

The following Monday, positions had hardened: £5 was the most J. H. Buckley was having. Tom Needham, an Oldham man, had been in their minds the previous week as a cornet player, and John Schofield had written to him to ask about his terms. They now concluded, in the face of J. H. Buckley's intransigence (I mean, he hadn't a single bargaining point, except he was there, and wouldn't go away), to ask Mr Needham to come as bandmaster and conductor.

Tuesday, 11 January, Thomas Needham, as he's now deemed, and quite right too at the price, is hired at the rate of £16 a year, and paid 2s 6d for his expenses between Oldham and Dobcross. With beer at tuppence a pint I don't know how he got through half a crown, but he did. The rail fare from Oldham Mumps to Dobcross Halt was 1s return. At the same meeting they decided to borrow £40 at 4 per cent over four years: they were determined to get a conductor on their terms, even if it cost. This loan was from Ephraim May, who had a sweet shop on Platt Lane within living memory; a 'warm man', who was good for a loan of a pound at a penny a week interest for any of his workmates at the foundry. He bought Platt Lane Farm, with six acres of land, for £400 in 1906.

A week later (we're back with the minutes now) things were getting desperate. Tom Needham hadn't materialised, and Shaw Singleton was being canvassed for his terms as conductor and solo cornet; Thomas Schofield to act as conductor pro tem.

In February they tried Sam Radcliffe '... on the terms he mentioned subject to the band attending practices'. They had more wit than I did some seventy years later when I asked the committee whether I should go ahead and book a certain man for bandmaster'.

'Go ahead,' said one bandsman and committeeman, 'but I know one man that'll probably wind a tenor horn round his neck inside a fortnight.'

They were sparky times, and it wasn't doing the committee's peace of mind any good. By 2 February 1899, they were offering J. H. Buckley the same terms he'd had the previous year … 'his term to expire at the end of the year'. So we can assume he'd still been in the middle during 1898, at £5, and the committee was stewing in their own bile. They printed 1,000 balance sheets, so the skirmishing was on firm ground.

A fearsome but scholarly contemporary of Buckley – the Reverend William Simpson, vicar of Dobcross, 1897

They had another go for Shaw Singleton in March 1899, but it looks as if he could smell the brimstone, because they were still making noises in his direction in May. J. H. Buckley had got his £8 in February '... his term to expire at Christmas or December 31st Dec 1899'. And on 26 Jaunary 1900 is the entry: 'That James H. Buckley be appointed bandmaster for the year 1900 at the sum of £8.0.0. per annum'.

I think Mr Buckley made his point, and it's an unfair aspect of band politics that if you belong to the village you'll find it that much harder to have your talents valued and respected. Buckley became landlord briefly of *The Nudger Inn*, and that together with the engagement of Shaw Singleton as conductor at 7s a practice (not bandmaster of course), persuaded him to retire with the dignity of an embattled winner.

It's also unfair, but true, that from 1901 the band surged forward in an extraordinary way. A ladies' committee took charge of raising money for the instrument fund, a new uniform was ordered and paid for, and a fine one it was, blue with silver frogging, and the short-peaked kepi associated with the Rifle Volunteers.

Concert after concert was given. There was one in the Mechanics Institute, Uppermill (next village down the valley) which raised £20, equivalent probably of £600 in 1975.

The medals and the baton were won at Miles Platting Contest in

The band in 1905   *Right* Minutes of September 1903

Committee Meeting held Sept 16th /03

Chairman Mr W Damforth

The following motions were made and passed

1) That the minutes of last meeting be passed as read

2) That A. E Booth go to Almondbury (Singers) to see the singers in regard to the Concert

3) That we allow him 5/ for his expenses

4) That the Secretary write to Mr J Shaw (conductor) to see what dates he has open in October

5) That A. E Booth & F. May see Marshall Bloadlent in regard to his subscription

6) That the medals & Baton be put on view in J Brierleys window

7) That we adjourn till Monday Sept 20th /03

Special Meeting held Sept 22nd /03

Chairman Mr W Damforth

The following motions were made and passed

1) That an acknowledgement be sent the Hand Bell ringers in regard to the Concert

2) That Mr John Shaw be engaged for the Concert

3) That we ask Mrs S Wigley & J. E Sykes to sing at the Concert

4) That we ask Mr A Pogson if he will accompany the Singers.

August and the prize money was shared among the bandsmen. The 'ringers' were a team of handbell ringers.

The Christmas Draw of 1903 was a noble do: first prize was a two guinea hamper, second prize a load of flour and third prize a ton of coal. There were fourteen prizes altogether, the smallest being half-pound of tobacco (2s 6d) which you could hardly provide for £4 today.

Charlie Anderson was appointed conductor; he came from Oldham, and worked as a mechanic in Bradbury's Sewing Machine Shop there. He played cornet with Besses' o' th' Barn Band, and found time to play in the orchestra pit at the Empire Theatre, Oldham. He was to conduct the band right through to 1923. The formidable Booth Roberts was bandmaster, and John Schofield secretary.

I don't think anyone has explained the powerful optimism, like the flush on a consumptive's cheek, that possessed Great Britain in the years leading up to the Great War. The nation's loss of 21,774 young men in the subjugation of the Boers seems to have been looked on as a noble sacrifice, rather than as evidence that beetles can dodge boots, and even drill holes in them as they dodge. One thing certain is that the bustle and solidity, the certainty and vigour of that time is still comforting in the faded sepia of their portraits.

Mrs Mary Schofield (Jack Warper's wife) and Mrs Booth Roberts, and all the wives of the senior members of the band, set up an enormous two-day bazaar, which was held in Platt Lane School in 1905. Beautiful china tea services with gold lettering celebrating the band and the event, were ordered.

The young end of the band, plus wives and daughters, would rehearse plays in the band room and present them for the benefit of the band in Delph and Uppermill Mechanics' Institutes. Mrs Cullen recollects *Waiting for the Verdict* and *Lancashire Lass* among their successes; she also remembers a big hearty girl who had the task of fainting into a gentleman's arms, which she did so convincingly that she carried both hero and a nearby door clean away.

There was nobody left out that wanted to be in: the village lads thought it a privilege to go to practice and hold up the music for the men. Nearly every bandsman lived in the village, and it was their boast that they could call and hold a band practice in one hour flat.

The band still played occasionally for the Volunteers (now the

Charlie Anderson

6th, since the embarrassing moment at Huddersfield), but they were virtually homeless, except for the little band room, where they practised on Tuesday and Thursday evenings and Sunday mornings, and where small meetings could be held.

Now, right on the top of Lark Hill (and the larks do sing there still) was a fairground, run and owned by a family called Kelsey. People used to come from considerable distances in wagonettes, to enjoy the Pennine air on Sundays and holidays; children could use a boating pool, and there were swings, see-saws, and a roundabout. The café was a solid wooden building, single storey. In 1907 Kelsey decided to get out, and the band bought the café, for £12. They cleared a plot of rough ground at the top of the village, dismantled the hut, carried it down the hill by horse-lorry, wheelbarrow and main force, and re-erected it on the new site. Perhaps this seems a small thing; if it does, just try carrying 10ft x 10ft sections of 5/8 tongue and groove boarding, half a mile down rough tracks and lanes. The job wasn't done without a good deal of swearing and sweat and ill-feeling, it wasn't enough that they practised three times a week, every night for months bandsmen and supporters hurried in for their teas, and then out again to labour on the building. A bowling green was laid in front of the new building, a

John Schofield　　　　　　　　　　　　　　　The commemorative crockery

piano acquired; gallons of cream and maroon paint laid on, a stillage installed, and finally the band was home. They had a club, a social centre (ladies by invitation only, until World War II, when a wife in pursuit of an errant husband refused to be turned out, thus piercing for ever Dobcross's own male purdah), a place where concerts could be held, meetings, practices, all the band activities under the one roof.

Not long after it was up, young Billy Schofield saw flames leaping below their house in the direction of the club. It was actually a gas street-lamp afire, but his yell had his brother Frank and dad out of bed and down Crib Lane before they could think. Mary Schofield had had the new club for breakfast, tea and supper for longer even than a band-wife's patience could take: 'I hope it burns to the bottom!' she offered her departing menfolk.

They soon joined the Club & Insitute Union, and by 1911, it was the Dobcross Band Club & Workingmen's Institute, as it is today. This transformation needn't all have been in the credit column: workingmen's clubs can be contentious places, citadels of male pride, whereas at best the band is the village's pride. To this day women can't be full members of a CIU affiliated club, and we've seen how the support of the wives weaves into the band's story. Nowadays we have several young women playing in the band (unthinkable even before the last war), and their voice and vote in

The band in 1911

band affairs is as strong as anyone's; but the CIU rule persists in club matters. The social side, the bowls, snooker, cards, darts, also tends to exclude women, and it has the effect too of splitting the membership ... especially if the band's on hard times and doesn't look very impressive. Clubs also finance their amenities largely through the sale of beer, and this, of course, was something quite new to the band. Bar receipts in the last quarter of 1910 totalled £83 13s 1d and the second quarter of 1912 saw the takings rocket to £139 10s 11d. Nowadays we have a couple of fruit machines, which more than earn their keep (as much as £30 a night), but even in the early days there was an infuriating, and probably illegal, machine on which for a penny you could juggle large steel balls into numbered holes. If you had the reflexes of Muhammad Ali you could get a free go ... it was called 'The Clown', and made clowns of many of us.

There are several bands which include 'Temperance' in their title, and I'm sure they earn it, but sober observation tells me that many bandsmen are second only to furnacemen in the matter of thirst. A friend and neighbour tells me that as a child she would sometimes get the job of finding her father in whichever of the five village pubs he might be.

'Has your mother sent you?'

'No Dad, it's me that wants you home.'

'Right lass, I'll come now.'

Many bands resist the idea of having a bar where they practise, and certainly a pint pot under the chair is a sign of a poor band. Much later, in the sixties, I think there was a serious struggle between the interests of the club in general and those of the band and I suppose it's worth noting that the slaughter of the 1914–18 War and the wretchedness of the twenties did less harm to the band than the tinsel never-never prosperity of the property-owning democracy.

A great jazzman said that your true jazz player was a 'working class of a man', and it seems to apply to brass bandsmen as well. Today we have a director of a small winding mill, five schoolteachers, an executive engineer with the Post Office, and one with the Water Board. But I think it's safe to say that they retain and respect the values of working-class life as much as the joiners, electricians, millworkers and panel beaters alongside whom they play. Both the stamina, the patience and application, and the need to excel come from an acceptance of hard and confining physical work. It's rough to come home in your dirt, have a quick wash and change, grab your tea, and then go straight out to a gruelling two-hour practice: you have to be tough, and you have to want to do it very much. With us, there is certainly also a deep devotion to the value of a small and cohesive community: not just any old band, it has to be Dobcross. A good player is a man to respect. During the first war, Billy Schofield, son of John, got the sack from Gatehead Mill for taking time off to go with the band to the Crystal Palace Contest, and his boss was generally considered a contemptible fool.

Only a well-heeled parent can consider or will consider buying a decent flute, say, or a fiddle, for a child to discover its musical abilities: but if you live in Dobcross, and there's a cornet free, you'll get a chance to 'get a note', and honk away in the Wednesday beginners' class. Eddie Tweedy plays B flat bass now with the 'A' Band, and he didn't start until he was nearly forty. Mrs Cullen recalls being brought up in a house in Crib Lane at the turn of the century, with father John Schofield and two brothers, all cornet-tists, and Ossie Langfield, bass drummer on the floor below, and that's one house. Later Mrs Howarth raised Norman (tenor horn), Herbert (soprano cornet), Stanley (trombone) and Jack (euphonium), all in one little house at the top of Long Lane; no running water, but they had and have music.

Certainly the biggest single influence ever on the band was Jimmy Platt, appointed bandmaster in 1923. He was born in Diggle, son of a euphonium player and learnt his music from Jack Carter, of Besses. He played cornet with Diggle Band, and his brother, Fraser, was there on baritone. They and two other young members of the Diggle Band used to make a few bob playing for dances; the word went out that the committee, father among, didn't altogether approve. Sooner than have trouble Fraser and another bandsman took their instruments and uniform in on the Monday, to the high indignation of the band elders. This is a controversy that still goes on: most bandsmen will tell you that playing dance music, pop or jazz spoils your lip and style for brass band music. My guess is that players with a harder tone and more flamboyant and individual approach will incline to favour dance music rather than that good players are spoilt by playing the wrong music. In any case, I offer Fraser and Jimmy as solid examples that both kinds of music can come from the same bell ends: both were top-class brass players.

Jimmy Platt

36

The result of the Diggle kerfuffle was that Fraser ended up with the Delph Band. After the war, Jimmy also joined the Delph, after which he finally came to us.

He was six foot one, very straight-backed, quiet-spoken and steady of manner. Like most of the village men he was recruited into the Duke of Wellington's Regiment, but was transferred to the Flying Corps when that was formed. 'The Dukes' was also the Territorial Army unit in the Oldham Area (the TA replaced the Rifle Volunteer companies after the Boer War) and when they were put on active service formed the 1st and 2nd Seventh Battalions. This was the insensitive 'Pals' Regiments' system, whereby the generals sent the young men of an entire district to the shambles at the same time.

Jimmy was a joiner by trade, and finished his working life at Jack Smith's undertaker's and joiner's shop in Platt Lane. (Matter of fact, he got Jack to take the big drum in 1933). He could be brutally dismissive ('Take it out of here and come back when you can get a—note out of it'), but he couldn't have held those assorted and rampageous characters together as he did during the long years he was bandmaster without a bumping measure of shrewd wisdom and perception.

Gel Littlewood was for many years a butcher in Dobcross, and the finest I ever came across in two continents; he was wounded in the leg at the Somme, and sent back to the regimental depot to convalesce. As a sergeant, he was put in charge of a billet, and of course it had to be the regimental band in there, half of Dobcross Band among. He later recalled with some indignation trying to set them on to window-cleaning: by the time he'd stumped round one side of the hut with his gammy leg, the Dobcrossers on the other side had departed quietly for the day.

Clarence Farr, who learnt cornet with Jimmy Platt, remembers how Jimmy urged him to take part in the Junior Section of a Slow Melody Contest at the Armoury in Ashton under Lyne. Slow Melodies are contests between individual players. Clarrie was just sixteen, a big lad for his age, and petrified. The colliers of Ashton took one look at the opposition to their own favourites and began to bellow 'Get off! Th'art too old!' His father had had the foresight to bring Clarrie's birth certificate, which he brandished and boldly demanded order for his son, but after a start like that, Clarrie didn't figure.

On the Sunday following, Jimmy Platt sent a neighbour, Charlie

Whiteley, round to Clarrie's house to ask him to play his solo at the band concert that night.

Jimmy brought up his family in a house at the end of Sugar Lane which forms a group with other dwellings known as Knoll; and Mrs Harold Buckley recalls with pride and affection that every year on 23 May, from when she was a child, Jimmy would walk quietly round to their yard and play a birthday hymn for her on his cornet.

In the same year that he was appointed bandmaster, the band began to employ Joe Jennings as professional conductor, at 30s a session.

Joe Jennings

Joe was solo euphonium with Shaw Band (just over the hill on the Oldham side of us), and had been with them in 1909 when they won Crystal Palace, W. Rimmer conducting. He was a cobbler in Cheetham Hill, a reserved man, of whom the band were just a little in awe: when Billy Percival raised his cornet and a hard-boiled egg fell out of the bell end and rolled across the floor, hilarity was in the recollection rather than in the moment. In contrast with Jimmy, who was several times censured by the committee for his crisp and sometimes lurid commentaries on the band's errors during Sunday park jobs and concerts ('Read music? you couldn't read the Sunday paper' … 'You're too idle to shiver when you're cold: blow the bloody thing'), Joe was restrained. The worst Clarrie Farr can recollect Joe saying was to Jack Byrnes when they were rehearsing the well-worn contest-piece 'Mephistopheles'. Jack had said privately before they sat down that he was going to 'give it some clog' tonight, and as the cornets blared into the first few bars, Joe spotted the culprit straight off. He stopped them, leaned forward to fix Jack on front row cornet and offered: 'You brigand'.

Joe was also well informed on the history and theory of music, which is unusual even among today's bandsmen, and sometimes gave lectures in the club on Sunday evenings.

The band hadn't figured in a contest since 1913 when Charlie Anderson took them to the Chapel en le Frith Selection Contest, and now, the bandsmen back from the army, and a new generation in charge, they were ready for the long haul up to eminence. Jack Schofield had had to have his teeth out, and it brought him to tears that he would never play again. Billy Woodcock was still on cornet, while Harry Ramsden was now on one E flat bass (he'd won the euphonium medal at Chapel en le Frith) and Jack Roberts was on the other. These are the only players still there from the pre-war band, and they look as if they've had the innocence taken out of them.

Their first contest with Joe Jennings was at Buxton, and they were apprehensive men. Harry Ramsden fingered the battered old bass as they went onto the stand and muttered: 'I'll fettle [clean] this if we've to do it again.' (They were green). We were drawn first, and Clarrie Farr had to leave before the results, for a dance-job at the Oddfellows Hall in Oldham. At ten o'clock, Jack Byrnes came into the dance hall with the great silver cup in one hand, raised

Before and after World War I: Harry Ramsden

... and after World War I: Billy Woodcock

Before ...

... and after World War I: Jack Roberts

it high for Clarrie to see, and gave one wave of his cap. They'd won. In the same year they won the Oldham Park Contest and came fourth in the Belle Vue Contest in Manchester. The Belle Vue Contests are the premier contests; if you've won there nobody can dispute your excellence. They're all-comers contests, no regional selection as at the Albert Hall; the best salute the best, and the humblest can enter.

Bands were first divided into classes there in 1912, until World War I decimated our ranks, and it wasn't until 1931 that the bands had recovered enough to make it possible to have two classes again. In 1931 two 'Marching' classes were also introduced–one for deportment, and one for the march itself; a gap of fourteen years, mournful and eloquent as a war memorial. Joe Jennings was ambitious for the band, and through his contacts they began to get park jobs. Harry Hirst was secretary, and he, Jimmy Platt, and the treasurer ran the band. No committee was deemed necessary, although the club itself had one of course. Decisions were taken 'in the band', with Jimmy as boss. This is sad for me as historian, looking for verifiable dates, but the band flourished all right. If you want to be legalistic or formally democratic, the arrangement probably wasn't right. It wouldn't be possible, for instance, for even a majority of the bandsmen to turn the band in a direction they

The band in 1922

46

favoured unless Jimmy thought the same way. However, he was a superb cornettist, and he was bonded into the village by now. He lived for the band, and the band respected him: he probably had an understanding of what was wanted, which dates they could take, which contests they could enter without bringing themselves to their knees, better than any other man.

Joe Jennings was capable of making them work till they rocked. One time he was driving Fraser Platt, on euphonium (Joe's own instrument of course), back and forth over the same short section.

'Again' he iterated, 'Again ...' Suddenly he stopped and said:

'You know Fraser, you look as if you could just do with a pint.' Fraser's tongue passed over his lip at the recollection:

'I could an' all.'

'Well you shall have one, at the break.' Came the break, Joe ordered his own half of Seth Senior's mild (2d.) and 'Whatever Fraser drinks'.

'Pint of Tetley bitter,' said the steward cheerfully, '7d.'

The experience scarred Joe, and later, when he saw Fraser drinking bottles with Squire Ashley (soprano cornet) during a break at a contest, he demanded to know what was all this?

'Ah,' said Fraser, unblinking, 'I don't know whether it's true or not, but I did hear the water this brewery uses comes from a stream that passes through a graveyard.' Joe quickly abandoned his half of mild and went to get himself a bottled ale.

'You did right to tell him.' said Squire Ashley, as he teemed Joe's half into his own pot.

There's an attractive tradition in Saddleworth, for the young men to adventure out. Sometimes it'll be on the trawlers out of Hull, professional rock-climbing, map-making expeditions, and even gathering reindeer-moss has figured. In the late twenties and the thirties, when the Depression was creeping over the industrial countries, many had no choice but to go. Bandsmen were luckier than most, in that they would be offered jobs by works and colliery bands. It's probably healthy for a young man to shake his wings in the world before he settles down to responsibilities, but for a man born in Saddleworth the exile can be dismal. Squire Ashley's adventure was briefer than most: he had a small holding and a few hens just under Saddleworth Moor, and was never much inclined for wages. He'd no moral objection to drawing the dole, however, and was caught in a crossfire when Cresswell Colliery offered him a place in the band, plus job. One look at Cresswell Colliery's underground convinced him that Offenbach did these things better, and he was back in time for practice the next day.

'They've no whitewash on the walls', he said, 'I don't fotch coal awhoam: them as wants coal'd better fotch for theirsel.'

One night in 1934 Squire Ashley tumbled down an unmarked and unlit roadwork at the bottom of Nicker Brow (a steep and narrow pathway hard enough to negotiate in broad daylight). He broke his jaw, and never played seriously again. However, he did take part in the beginnings of the band's days of greatness, which is only right, as he was a soprano player of great quality. At a contest on Whit Saturday in Southport we came fourth among such gaints as Foden's Motorworks, and Cresswell Colliery. I hope it's understood what Goliaths these men were to our Davids: in times when jobs were short, firms supporting a band could tempt the best players into their ranks, and they were grateful for the chance of a steady job. They could employ the most famous and respected musical directors, while we were scratting for thirty bob a practice for ours. Harold Buckley joined us on trombone in 1933, and as he puts it, 'We could run the band on a pound a week.' At Southport Squire Ashley, in his bounding elation at our success, went among the monumental bass players and brooding trombonists of the Championship bands enquiring how they liked their eggs boiled.

At a contest in Reddish, where there was a top prize of £12, they had their first taste of the envy and malice that their rising star would provoke: the public there, and the other bands, considered Dobcross were playing unfairly below their class, and they were booed as they went on. For once, Joe Jennings felt he'd misdirected the band, and muttered sardonically that they were playing for third prize at best. The band weren't used to that kind of a reception, which is usually reserved for the arrogance of champions, or a perverse adjudication, and they were glum. They won the £12.

After the 1931 win, the band was on the home straight. Jimmy Platt's son Bob joined the band in 1932. His father taught him and his brother Harry music; and if Jimmy could be sharp with the band, he was savagely strict with his sons: they were made to play, no choice. My grandfather was a bully to my father, and the custom of the times approved hard authority in a parent as it accepted severity from the police and the army (well, towards the poor). Those who talk of some special violence today should spend

Squire Ashley

Dobcross Prize Band, winners of the Dr Fawsitt Cup and Oldham Chronicle Cup, 1931

a few hours looking over newspaper files. Neither Harry nor Bob were cowed by their father's harshness, in fact as he grew up, Bob could give as good as he got, from his father or anyone else for that matter. Harry learnt cornet although he didn't keep it up; Bob was, and is, in the first rank of cornet players.

I suppose it figures: when Fraser left Diggle Band, sooner than have trouble with the committee (of which their father was a prominent member) over their little dance band, Jimmy stuck it out and defied them. Bob has never pushed his own son into music, and he's a careful, attentive teacher, appreciative of effort and encouraging. I know–he's taught my son.

The line-up of the 1935 band was impressive. Many of them were Jimmy's pupils, all of them were his friends. Harold Buckley remembers it as the happiest band he was ever in. Although Jimmy was strict on the podium, and Joe Jennings exacting, the atmosphere was one of trust, confidence, and ready humour. Bob Platt was librarian, and was required to set out music to be practised once, then scooped up again, not to be seen until the concert. 'I'll stop you gazing round the club during a concert,' said Jimmy. Every man in that Band was a good sight-reader ... had to be.

If evidence is required of the standards they were reaching, consider the number of them that later joined top-flight bands: Bob Platt, Yorkshire Copperworks, Crossley Carpets, Brighouse & Rastrick; Jack Philips, CWS Manchester; Herbert Howarth, Co-op and Fairey; Jack Urmston, Sankeys; Brian Broadbent, Black Dyke; Stanley Whiteman, CWS Manchester; Jack Byrnes, Brighouse & Rastrick; George Gibson, Wingates.

Four new basses were bought 'in the brass' (not silvered), and the band was entered in the top section of the Belle Vue Contest, 3 May 1935, the test-piece being Percy Fletcher's 'Epic Symphony'. Percy Fletcher was the first composer of note to take the possibilities of the brass band sound seriously, and 'Epic' is appallingly difficult.

The general standard of musicianship and playing is almost certainly much better in the brass band movement today than it was before the war. The attention of serious composers (as distinct from 'light music' composers, and self-taught bandsmen), like Eric Ball, Malcolm Arnold, Gilbert Vintner and Elgar Howarth, testing the capacities and sensibilities of the players, and the range of the instruments, combined with the serious support of the education authorities, arts associations, and councils, have combined to raise both the numbers of people playing and the quality of the music played.

Before the war the middle-class suburbanite looked down on the rough-spoken bandsman for his devotion and his lack of status; now we are patronised in opaque reviews in the quality press. One of these managed to devote a paragraph to explaining how brass bands are in a different pitch to orchestras, which we are not; we were when his reference book was written, but he hasn't got round to talking to bandsmen yet.

Bob Platt was astonished when he played 'Epic' with Brighouse & Rastrick in 1974; it was difficult enough for them now, 'And there we were, a little village band, taking on the world with it!'

3 July 1935. The band charabanc, with five more for the village supporters following on chugged down through Uppermill, Mossley, Ashton, Denton, to the King's Hall, Belle Vue. It was a crushingly hot day, airless and humid. Joe Jennings was to conduct them, but had Denton Original to conduct first, his home town band. He passed out on the stand from the oppressive conditions. However, Dobcross must still have had some Pennine air in the tubes of their instruments to refresh him. 'This is your chance,' he

The Cup ...

... And the band that won it

said to Fraser Platt as they got onto the stand, 'if ever you had one.'

It was the Golden Jubilee of the July Belle Vue Contests, and belonged, without any trace of a doubt, to Dobcross Band. As the afternoon wore on, neighbours in the village were hastily opening doors if someone passed: 'Have you heard how they've got on?'

The result was first, Dobcross Band; second, Barrow Iron & Steelworks; third, Grimethorpe Colliery.

There was a cup, and £30 to be shared out; they were the Champions of Champions.

They were now the premier band for many a long mile about; no longer the loyal hard-working little group of villagers, more like battle-hardened veterans, into whose ranks it was a privilege to enter.

Judges in the smaller contests are normally men who have been in banding a long time, and they're naturally anxious not to make rank fools of themselves by rating a Champion band below some raggedy bunch of lads who get together for a beer and a blow every second Thursday. Any clue is a help, and bands are not above dropping a broad hint, as, for instance, playing a march known to be theirs alone (I'm not saying there aren't marked differences between the greatest bands, in tone, approach and emphasis, but even a judge is permitted a quiet smile now and then). Dyke have their own march, 'Queensbury', Brighouse, 'Ilkley Moor'–ours was 'High Command'. Sammy Schofield, on solo baritone with us until he emigrated to Australia found the march out there, bought a full score, and sent it home for the band.

We also had the distinction of being the only band to march up to a contest stand playing a hymn tune: the judge (a Dobcross man) was duly impressed, and awarded us first prize; of course it may have been that he had prior information, though I've never had it sworn to.

Lesser bands had to beware of losing their good players if Dobcross was a man short and Jimmy put the word out to secretary Arthur Thornton; because not only did the invitation to join come from a Championship band, but also there was the powerful community feeling, the solid support of the village and the security of their own club–the very qualities that grip and hold a bandsman from the conductor's first kind word, through the shared disasters and treasured triumphs, to an honoured grave. Nemesis was hovering over these proud men, but she hovered a marvellous long time before she struck.

Another nemesis was loading her thunderbolts over in the Third Reich, and perhaps a good illustration of the difference between a village and a works band, particularly at that time, can be seen in Bob Platt's experiences in 1939. Work was short, and Bob had taken a job in Hull, with British Oil and Cake Mills, and was also in their band. They did a lot of park jobs in the summer, and were playing at Scarborough Peasholm park when a representative of Yorkshire Copperworks asked him did he fancy a job nearer home?

The band in 1937

Which he did, if only to calm his mother's anxieties about the bachelor conditions he was living in. The job was in Leeds, and he could be home any weekend, so he became a capstan-lathe operator ... for which he had no special skill, but Tim Wood (horn player, now a manager with the same firm) was a good mate, and could pull Bob through and do his own job with the other hand.

There was a band rule that you couldn't play with another band while you were working for, and playing with, Yorkshire Copperworks.

Bob was home for the weekend, and went to support Dobcross at the Sale Contest. Thirty-eight bands were entered, and if you count, say, fifteen minutes a band, you get an idea of what an occasion it was: more than nine hours of solid music. Dobcross was drawn next to last, and Frank Taft (cornet) and Harold Buckley (trombone) had a dance band date in Oldham which meant they had to leave before the band went on. It was inconceivable that Bob could let his friends play a cornet short, so he sat in ... in any case nobody would think twice if he saw Bob Platt sitting among the Dobcross cornets. They went on the stand at twenty past eleven.

The Monday morning, he made it to work at 7.30 am, feeling pretty virtuous about it too. There was no time-card for him in the rack: just a note to see the manager before he started work. He got the bullet: somebody had managed to report his playing at Sale between 11.20 pm Saturday and 7.30 am Monday morning. At Belle Vue, after the war, he was sitting watching the contest with Harold Buckley, and they asked:

'When are you coming back to us?'

'I've had six and a half years to think about that,' said Bob genially. He was not a man to bear a grudge.

The band just about held together during the war. Bert Howarth was taken prisoner early on, George Gibson and Bob Platt were abroad most of the war, Edwin Cooke was killed flying with the RAF, Billy Orcher was in the navy, Stanley Potter in the RAF, Fred Mellor was killed fighting in the army, Frank Taft killed in the navy, Walter Cox was in the marines, and Douggie Haigh was a sergeant-major in the army. But many were able to come home on leave and have a blow; the new mobility also meant that visiting professionals would sit in. One Covent Garden player, William Brownbill, who later joined Jack Jackson's Dance Band, was a visitor who took intense pleasure (and gave it) in renewing his connection with the taproot of brass music.

One man who probably did more than anyone to keep a nucleus going was Albert Williams. He became secretary in 1940. A mild, upright and absolutely righteous man, he could suffer the most outrageous, boozy or awkward character, provided it served the band. When a bandsman keeled clean over in the snow after too many 'footings' (neighbourly drinks) as they played round the village through Christmas Eve and Morning, giving his trombone an extra curve, there was no reproach from Albert; he simply set about getting the instrument repaired. If somebody was short for the rent, it was always to Albert they turned. If I seem to suggest that bandsmen, even our bandsmen, are drunken wastrels to a man, it's a foul slur: they are, thank God, as other men. Only more so.

This is Frank Knott and his wife behind the bar; they were stewards from 1945-52. Frank kept the beer with dedicated passion, and he and his wife were a legend of kindliness–a bandsman hurrying in off shift would be offered soap and towel and 'Have you had a bite to eat?' During their stewardship the club was known as 'The Gluepot', and Frank was probably the only steward in the history of the Club and Institute Union to be called before the committee

Frank Knott and his wife behind the bar of the old club

for making too much trading profit. Three scores were bought specially for them: 'Happy Wanderer', 'Silver threads among the gold' (for their wedding anniversary), and 'Rudolph the Red-nosed Reindeer' (for reasons only colour photography would reveal, and certainly not his many friends).

When he became too ill to carry on as secretary in 1964, Albert Williams sent for me and asked me to take over; and I took the job on as a kind of nightmarish privilege. I don't think I did it very well, but I like to think I repaid his trust and kept the money straight … ish. He was an honourable man.

The men who came back from the war were not the boys who went; where the first war erased a generation and proved their convictions to be cruelly false, the next gave a taste, however illusory, of a new freedom. Dobcross's reputation, plus the players' own loyalty, brought them back. Jimmy was still in his prime; he had a sturdy committee made up of non-playing men in their late thirties and early forties: George Brierly, Eddie Gore, Ernie Battersby, Tom Hague (president). But the times had changed, we even said so, though we'd yet to have proof of it.

A concert at the Mechanics' Institute, Uppermill

The band continued to win the odd contest (Cadishead, Bury, Wigan) and to give excellent concerts.

On Whit Saturday, 1951, Jimmy had heard a mutter that some of the players had had offers from Mossley Band, and planned to leave. They played for the church procession at Lydgate, at the other end of Saddleworth. Afterwards, Jimmy, George Gibson and Albert Williams got the band together and asked was the rumour true? Eight men reluctantly admitted they'd been thinking on the subject. 'Right' said Jimmy, 'you can finish now.' One third of the band at a swipe; and they still turned out a full band for Whit Friday a week later.

The sense of aristocracy in the band persisted: past victories were vivid in the mind, and we had trained and supplied players to champion bands. Jack Howarth told me that in 1961-2, the twelve top bands in Great Britain each had at least one player from Saddleworth. When George Gibson was demobbed from the air force and returned to the club, he couldn't get a blow. He was later to do for the band what Jimmy Platt did in 1923–hoist them up by his bootstraps: in 1946, nobody wanted to know.

Jimmy was a revered figure, in his white gloves, blue frock coat, with bandmaster's sash, marching before the band in their maroon uniform with black and gold trimmings, and the high military collar. His fifty years' service with the brass band movement was celebrated in 1955 and he was made a life member of the National Brass Band Club.

Probably the most awkward man, and certainly one of the most talented musicians that ever belonged to Dobcross, was Joe Wrigley (Joe Puff as they called him, though seldom to his face). I knew him in later years, when he was a dry and acidulous man. I asked him his opinion of a conductor we'd acquired during one desperate sequence: 'I layfed' he said ('I laughed').

Joe joined the band in 1905, and played trombone for us off and on over the years: off because of his wayward temperament, on because he was brilliant at it. He could (and did) ask for more money as he walked onto the bandstand if the mood took him. At a club concert he was to play a duet with Jimmy Platt, and when Jimmy felt that his lip might go he turned his bell to Bobby, playing second man down ... the normal way to ask someone to take over. Hearing the (marginally) different tone, and possibly feeling that

The news of Jimmy's reward

LIFE MEMBERSHIP FOR JIMMY PLATT

DOBCROSS BAND CLUB was filled on Saturday evening, when members paid tribute to Mr. Jimmy Platt, the musical director, who has been connected with the brass band world for over 50 years. On behalf of the members, Mr. Hervey Rhodes, M.P., presented him with the honorary life membership award and badge of the National Brass Band Club of Great Britain, and a cheque and a writing set from the Dobcross club.

Councillor C. B. Hopkinson presided, and in introducing Mr. Rhodes said that they had assembled that evening to honour a son of Diggle who had devoted over half a century to brass bands and was still giving his best.

Mr. Rhodes referred to Bandmaster Platt's long and faithful service to Dobcross Band. He was a man they could be proud of in Saddleworth.

A lot of changes had taken place between the two world wars, and one of these was the replacement of horse-drawn vehicles by the motor-coach.

"I have recollections," said Mr. Rhodes, "of standing with my relative Hamlet Wood, on a Whit Friday morning and seeing bandsmen in horse-drawn waggonettes coming down Bills o' Jacks, at Greenfield from the other side of Yorkshire.

"It is half a century this year since I got my first cornet, but I couldn't blow it because it was clocked up. We put in in boiling water and you should have seen the quantity of tobacco juice and stale ale that came out of it."

Mr. Rhodes, who himself comes of a musical family said that there was plenty of scope in Saddleworth to bring out young bandsmen.

Many more happy years'

In making the presentation, and wishing Mr. Platt he said you are bound up with this band and I wish you very many more happy ...

MR. JIM PLATT

SUB-COMMITTEE APPOINTED FOR HOLIDAY PERIOD

In view of the fact that there be nex meeting of the Council or Council during August given to financial matters Period.

someone was trying to put one over on him, Joe stopped playing, dismantled and cased his trombone, and went home. Because he knew and respected Joe, Jimmy could understand this, even take pleasure in his running true to form. What he wouldn't understand was that not everybody had his long and glorious memory: it was not in his nature to stand down, or give way ... who else was there who loved and knew the band as he did?

In 1952 a breach occurred in the village which was not to be healed for fifteen years. I've hardly mentioned the churches of Dobcross so far, it's hardly my brief, but you may imagine that the Holy Trinity and the Congregational churches are very important, both as social centres and of course as places of worship. The church councillors, the vicar, and the senior members of the Congregational can represent village opinion with an accuracy that an MP might envy. Such people have always offered a leadership which has been hearkened, weighed, and possibly followed.

There have only been four vicars in the 100 years we're talking about, and Reverend Barlow, our present incumbent, is a comparative newcomer with only ten years' service. The band had always played for the Whit Friday processions, and whichever church hired them, they would make a donation back to funds out of the fee.

Left Joe Wrigley   Jimmy Platt leading the band

The Reverend Thomas was a small man, with dark watchful eyes and a will of cast steel; an autocrat, skilled in picking his way through the minefields of village politics. One council member describes him as having been well content with a committee of one: himself. He was relished as a man as much for his character, as for his considerable erudition. Harold Buckley remembers when the band was forming up one Whit, they suddenly noticed that they were the only band there ... they'd been booked for the church, and there was the Congregational about to follow on. Secretary Harry Hirst was despatched to explain to Reverend Thomas that they hadn't bargained for playing for the two.

'We were booked to play for you Mr Thomas,' said the secretary firmly.

'Ah,' said the Reverend Thomas, 'so you are; but these are our friends, whom we have invited to join us.'

The Coronation in 1953 was an event to be celebrated with a grand procession, which the band was expected to lead. However, they'd had a previous offer to play for £15 in Uppermill, and band feeling was strong for it. Ernie Battersby was club president, and realised the damage it could do if they persisted in abandoning Dobcross. Born in Leigh, a railway and coal town in Lancashire, I think he feels as I do coming from suburbia, more attached to the small community even than someone born to it. He went back and forth to Alvey Whitehead, secretary of the Coronation committee, trying to keep tempers down and the positions from hardening; Alvey even offered to better the Uppermill offer by £5, but suddenly the band set solid: they were not going to be Dobcross's private property. The churches and the band split apart, and stayed apart. Finally, in May 1961, Jimmy Platt retired.

Looking at the minutes for this period, I had the uneasy shock of seeing my own handwriting taking over from Albert Williams's. He gave twenty-one years' service, and knew what he was about; all I knew was that if I did the job properly, I wouldn't have the time to cope with it.

Even though the band was a shambles, with players hastily borrowed, concert programmes shuffled out and pieces rejected because we simply couldn't rehearse them, still there was a kind of embattled cosiness about that time.

The old club building was falling to bits ... one room was abandoned because it was over a permanent sump of water, the basses hung on the wall and you could see daylight through the metal.

Jimmy Platt's retirement

The committee (frequently me and Norman Howarth) met once a fortnight behind a tatty curtain at the end of the hut, usually to debate where the devil we could get players from, and often to rack our brains over the problem of a bandmaster. At the other end was the bar, and a few loyal club members telling the tale under fierce gas fires suspended from the iron struts of the roof. And yet we liked it, and the crack was good: Eric Hirst held court (as he still does) like a cross between natural monarch and court jester ('Oh I like Plymouth well enough, but dear me that ale ... you have to sup it quick before it drains out through the glass.' And on a bowling match: 'Bowls? Bowls? why, you'd need a sheepdog to round 'em up.')

The snooker table took up most of the middle of the one decent room, and had a waterproof (nearly) cover which was put on on concert nights so that beer pots could be put on it. You could talk to people in that old place ... in fact you had to, there were few seats in the centre, you were mostly sitting round the walls, so you either talked or stared somebody out of countenance. You needed no microphone to compere a concert, as we do nowadays. The last night in that building was a fine occasion, when supporters of the band, ex-bandsmen, people who'd been fond of the place, gathered for a last get-together. There were dialect recitations, Saddleworth songs, skits, musical items, all night and each by a different performer.

However, I'm getting before myself, and if you can bear it, I have to tell of the sad search for a conductor and for some bandsmen for him to conduct.

Some of the old players were still about: Bob, Jimmy's natural heir, didn't want to take over. Stanley Whiteman, a cornet player with us since 1947, took over first. But there wasn't much to take over, and his primary interest was with Mossley Band, at that time a progressive First Section band, who won the Edinborough Contest with him.

Then Harry Halstead, conductor of Littleborough Band helped out. Then Frank Greenhalgh, a cornet player with the band, but it

Club members in the old club   *Right* Jimmy Platt's memorial procession 1962

was only stick-wagging, and he knew it. Tell the truth that's all we were worth; Frank, and the few players we had, were all musicians of proveable quality, but we just weren't a band. Then Les Sutton, a teacher from Failsworth. I don't think Les knew any better than I what we were into, or what could be done, but I think he sensed better than anyone that the impetus had to come from the community itself: 'You don't realise what you've got here' were his words.

Then Bert Howarth, a Dobcross man. He'd played with us as early as 1931 and had developed into a class soprano player, playing with Mirr Lees and Fairey Bands. He's brisk, professional, go-getting: 'If you can't play my way, I'd rather not bother with you.' I only ever saw Bert show deference to a band once, and that was when an astonishing scratch band had been gathered at a local contest to fill a club concert date where we'd been let down.

Every man that sat down to play that night was a soloist in his own right; Herbert Howarth was the conductor. A hawker, who still plagues us on concert nights with his cockles and mussels, had no more sensitivity than to hoist his abominable basket and ease past the front of the band as they accompanied Philip McCann, at that time reigning champion cornet of Great Britain, in his solo 'The Nightingale'. As the basket reached Philip's raised

The majority of the band with Les Sutton

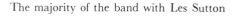

bell-end, with many an egregious nod and smirk from Mr Molly Malone, Bert turned briefly as you might imagine a cobra striking. I never heard the word, but Molly Malone turned back the way he'd approached, made a full circuit of the room, and shot out.

If ever there was a man for a time, and for that time, it was George Gibson. He was a sheet metal worker by trade, but music has gradually eased everything else out. I doubt if he has any letters after his name, and I suppose he's not a particularly erudite man, or even a natural player, but he started to give lessons at the Oldham Music Centre, at night school, and in various schools about 1960, and discovered his gift for and love of teaching brass band music. He's said to me: 'I don't think any child could get more out of a lesson than I do. I'd do it for nothing.' The Education Authority sent him on a course at Leeds once, in hopes of improving him. I inquired was it harmony? Musical history? Interpretation? The nearest thing to despair I've ever seen in him clouded his brow. 'Interpersonal ... relationships,' he said, with the eyes of a martyred saint. George is without question a born genius at getting people together. I've seen him offer wigs-on-the-green to a committeeman (Eddie Tweedy, bass player, ex-military policeman and Rugby forward, built like a brick bowls hut), and ten seconds after the meeting had broken up in disorder, the pair of them were

The band committee in the late sixties

exchanging pints like second row men after a rugged match.

The crazy thing is we couldn't see George's value at the time. During 1965-6 we graciously allowed him to take a beginners' class gratis for us (we had to get players from somewhere, and had no sort of a policy on the subject); we did vote him a briefcase after a year, however.

In fact did we but know it, the necessary shake-up was ruminating in the bowels of time. The club committee, also with their backs to the wall (I was also a member of that committee, and it was glum) had steeled themselves to borrow £10,000 from the brewers and build a new club.

The interim, homeless period, reaffirmed village backing in a comforting and endearing way. I'd only been in the village five years, and really didn't know my way about. In Saddleworth, whatever you want, you 'put the word out' … ask people you know to ask people they know. I'd found an appalling slum for the band to rehearse in: the floor was suspect, and the ceiling dubious, and it was mucky. Herbert Howarth took one brief look round, turned on

George Gibson   Right Eddie Tweedy

The Swan Inn, usually known as the 'Top House'

his heel and marched to the 'Top House' and asked Eric Swallow for the use of the top room of the pub. Eric was glad to let us have it, put no time limit on us, and never charged a ha'penny. Bert hated having anything to do with the organisation side, it wasn't, after all, his job, but he knew how to go about things in Dobcross.

By January 1967 we were having the band AGM in the new club which was bigger and better organised. There was a separate concert room and a storeroom for music (the "Band 'ole") uniforms and instruments: at first you could walk freely round from the snooker and games room and the lounge (the bar is in the middle) but it was soon seen that doors helped each activity.

The club itself, now almost entirely separate from the band, struggled at first (a defecting steward and some dubious accounts didn't help). They still paid the bandmaster, and were willing to help out with instrument repair in an emergency; but they got so alarmingly near the bottom of the barrel at first that we feared for our instruments, which had got themselves onto the club inventory. There are several references in the minute book to the 'Uniform Fund ' ... this is a measure of our fears: there were we (well, the band wives) raising money for the band, and the club's creditors

The new club

looking ominous. By having a separate fund we could at least claim it was ours. It was a bad time, but George had got the beginners' class up to sixteen, including several older men. This was our good fortune–men whose children were beginning to grow up and could glimpse the possibility of finally paying off mortgages, looked round for a hobby and found Dobcross Band. I mentioned Eddie Tweedy earlier, and he's worth it: seventeen stone of bull-neck enthusiasm. He hurtles back to practice from wherever his job with the Post Office takes him ... 300 miles is his record I think. Once he slipped a disc and was confined to bed. A fellow player called and enquired of Fiona, whether her father could be visited. He was conducted up-stairs, to find the warrior propped up in bed with five pillows, and Mrs Tweedy holding the music up, while he practiced the double bass.

Several of us were beginning to recognise what George could br-ing to the band, but it was actually George himself who made the points. Although there is no formal process for appointing a band-master the body of the band and the officers do have to agree, and a vote is then taken, which the club committee endorses. It could just as well be a committee decision, without consultation. We were paying £60 a year at that time, for two practices a week, concert and contest dates, so nobody was going to get rich. George stood up at the AGM and spoke with immense dignity:

'I don't imagine I'm anything special, but I'd like to take the job on. I think if we allow the youngsters to come on, give them a chance to play in the band as soon as they're proficient enough, then we'll have a band. It's no use expecting players to come here fully fledged, we've got to build. And I'll promise you this, within six months' time, we'll have a contesting band here. I came here in 1938 to Dobcross, and my heart's always been with this band, ever since. Just give me the chance to show what I can do, and in due course you can sack me or do whatever you've a mind to.'

And, as he was rejected in 1946, so was he in 1967.

At the same meeting a ladies' committee was formed. This in-cluded Mrs Herbert Howarth and other band wives (we now had five Howarths; my friend and neighbour Norman, on tenor horn, Bert in the middle, brother Stanley on trombone, Jack, who had come from Manchester Co-op on euphonium, and Bert's son, Bob, who was on cornet) and also Marjorie Fielding, a major acquisi-tion. Marjorie is a quiet woman, usually sombre, who knows everything and is known by everyone in the brass band movement throughout the north of England. I suppose one day she will take her rightful place as chairman of one of the brass band associations (the joint co-ordinating bodies in each area, which deal with registrations and contests) but for the moment she gives her time and work to whichever bands she has under her wing at the time. I have ties, scarves, clothes-peg bags, grubby curling raffle tickets, all manner of clutter she's used to extract my money, and most people who follow bands round here could say the same.

The major job for 1968 was to get the instruments into low pitch, which all bands were doing or have since done: that is, get them into the same pitch as orchestras use nowadays. Since brass bands were developing at the same time as the instruments themselves, and since we had special requirements as amateurs, a special type of instrument came to be conventional to brass bands. A professional will play two or more instruments, and give his days and nights to learning each one: brass, woodwind, string and percussion, each totally different, and valued for the contrast each with the other. A brass band is lucky to have one professional teacher,

An early nineteenth-century cornet

MACFARLANE'S CLAPPER SHAKE-KEY.

and so it was convenient to have a set of instruments which all (except the trombones) have the same sort of valves, and mostly play the same scale. (Yes, I do know about four-valve euphoniums and basses, and key-change cornets, and the E flat instruments, but these are exceptions). If you want to practice your double B, you can pick up a cornet score, and the tune will come out right; if you're getting older, and your lip no longer has the elasticity for the high eyeball-squeezers of the soprano, you can take up a baritone or a bass and still hold a place. If you pick up a flute, having learned the oboe, you can't even hold your face the same.

As these special instruments were developed, each with its three piston-valves (M Perinet's 'improved circular valve' seems to have been the first, about 1839, but Adolph Sax had been experimenting before this to simplify and improve the way air could go round a brass tube), so was the pitch established, and this was made mechanically easy for the player, where the violins and clarinets, say, depend on highly trained professional ears. And as we nowadays suspect that Mozart heard a different sound from his player's unvalved horn to the one Alan Civil produces so magically, so our instruments diverged from orchestral pitch. And, as serious composers were paying attention to us, it behoved us to pay attention to their ways. And what it meant was that every instrument (except the trombones) had to have more tubing, by means of short cylinders inserted in the ramifications (longer tubes equal lower range). And it cost.

The usual sales-of-work, concerts, draws, fairs were set agate, but the best was a 'Record Contest', plus potato pie supper (6d a plate) on 14 April 1967. The idea was that each of us would bring along his favourite brass band record to be played for the general company's pleasure, and a judge would award three modest prizes ('value to depend on entries') to the owner of the best. The entrance fee was 2s 6d. The occasion was social and fund-raising, rather than a major critical appraisal, and the judge, a bandsman, modestly declined a fee. However, since he was missing a good deal of the fun (hidden away in the band store-room so that he wasn't influenced by nods and winks from contestants), could he please have a pint brought in once in a while. This was agreed, and a potman appointed. What nobody had worked out was that records can take a little while to play through ... and no restrictions had been placed on length or number of entries. Some eighty entries were made, and our judge settled to his pint and his adjudication. Major contest piece followed march, followed tone poem, followed symphonic variations, followed hymn; the potato pie was long gone, and the lights were going out all over Saddleworth. The potman marched back and forth faithfully, until he was gripping the last pint the steward would part with. He went into the band store-room, to find your man spreadeagled peacefully on the floor, his notes about him.

'D'you want this last pint or not?'

'Oh,' said the judge, scrambling up and shaking his head clear, 'Is it over?'

By now, Eddie Stemp was secretary, a neat small man, with vaguely bashful eyes who provided (with the aid of Mrs Stemp) six players for the band.

The minutes of 23 July 1967 record that the band committee were exercised to know why they couldn't have every penny the contest had produced. With £34 in the fund and a double B to pay for, they had a right to be exercised. Uniforms were a problem, everything was a problem: but we did have a solid and devoted committee, and a hard-working ladies' committee. What we lacked, we gained on 13 August 1967. At a specially convened General Meeting, brought about by Herbert Howarth's resignation, George Gibson was elected bandmaster.

The band in 1969

He rapidly built up the beginners' class, brought in young players from the schools where he taught; by a mixture of dogged persistence and hilarious abuse he began to build both the numbers and the loyalty we needed. Some of his practices can be as good as a music-hall act 'Basses? you sound more like a delivery of Phimax', 'Now if you're taking music home to practise, don't put it on the piano and tell your Mum don't touch, I'll need it next week–look at it'), and simply because there was progress to be seen, supporters began to come to practise to sit quietly, or to offer help. Fraser Platt had retired, after fifty-two years' service with us; my old friends and neighbours who'd got me interested in the first place–Norman Howarth, Ernie Battersby, Bert Broadbent–had given over: we'd been down to six players, but now it was a band again.

By the autumn of 1968 we were contesting: Uppermill and Rochdale, two practices a week with extra ones for contests; fifty-two concert and parade engagements in 1967-8, and we'd raised and spent £532 18s 5d. And by 1970, we were winning. Best Local Band (£5) at Dobcross Whit Friday, Best Third and Fourth Section Band at Crompton.

At the 1970 AGM the idea of 'acquiring the services of a professional conductor' was raised (January) but it wasn't until September, with the Uppermill Contest looming, that it became urgent. The problem was that we had so much, the prospect of putting our precious basket of hard-won talent into the hands of some impervious and imperious outsider needed careful examination. In fact, there were two immediately possible men. Since we'd established our own contest in the village, Teddy Gray had been judge: he was first cornet in the Foden Band and was interested in conducting. We all knew him, and it's impossible not to like him: quiet, meticulous, firm and musically well-informed: his judge's notes are always both constructive and perceptive. The other possibility was Derek Broadbent: stroppy, flamboyant, individualistic, who conducted Slaithwaite (pronounced Slawit) over the Stanedge Cutting in Yorkshire. He'd been a military bandsman, pit orchestra trumpet, and had his own special line in malapropisms ('Comparisons are oblivious'), and was getting some glorious noise out of Slaithwaite Band. It turned out that Teddy wasn't available until the New Year, and so we didn't have to make the choice. My own purely personal feeling is that Derek is a rising star. He's a composer himself, and insists that he conducts for every mark and note; my observation is that when he conducts, especially in the richer scorings that particularly suit his talent, it sounds more so than when another conductor deals with the same piece. Slaithwaite got a four minute standing ovation for their playing of Dvorak's 'New World Symphony' at the Buxton Contest in 1970, Derek conducting.

He is at the time of writing conductor of the great Brighouse & Rastrick Band, and he hasn't finished yet.

In 1972 we took part in a TV film, and there was a nice piece of editing in it which illustrates neatly the contrast of character and experience between George Gibson and Derek Broadbent. Each was shown talking to his band in a motor coach thundering through the mountain rain on the way to a contest. First George: 'Now look, if you want a drink, by all means have a drink, but two halves is plenty. Once it's over you can have as many pints as you've a mind to. I'll buy you a pint myself, and pour it over your head if you want it.' Then Derek to Slaithwaite Band: 'Are you listening to me? because you should be: for heaven's sake watch the crotchets ...' They were never going to mix.

In fact the band did well in every way with Derek Broadbent: we came third in the Third Section, Northern Area Championship and bought a fine new uniform ... scarlet jacket, with black revers, and had a blazer badge made which showed our allegiance to Both Yorkshire and Lancashire:

We made a record for sale towards funds, and a radio programme on the early history of the band on 3 October 1971.

Minutes of Meeting held 4 Jan 1972.
Mr T. B. Hague in the chair.
Those present Messrs Woodhead, Schofield, Platt, Gibson, Peters, Baire, Jackson, Tweedy & Bottom.
   Mr W. Whyatt & Mr W. Platt attended in there capacity of VP.

1   That the minutes of the previous meeting be passed as a true and correct record.

2   It was proposed by Mr Woodhead and seconded by Mr Gibson that we ask Reynolds if they could match the terms offered by Stock & Chapman in connection with the purchase of 3 New Tenor Horns.

3   The treasurers report was passed unanimously.

4   The committee accepted Mr R. M. Devy's resignation from the Dobcross Band Management Committee.

The band badge

5   It was proposed by Mr Gibson and seconded by Mr Platt that we have a recut made of the recent gramophone record. The number to be ordered be 90.

6   It was suggested by Mr Woodhead that the band enter 4 contests in the early part of 1972. These being Rochdale, Mossley, Oldham & Belle Vue. Mr Gibson agreed to play B Bass.

The A. G. M. was fixed to the 13th Feb 1972.

8   It was again proposed by Mr Woodhead & seconded by Mr Tweedy that the Dobcross Junior Band be officially formed, under the guidance of Mr G. R. Gibson.

9   It was proposed by Mr Jackson and seconded by Mr Gibson that minute 5 of the meeting held on the 10th June 1971 be recinded (ie No more female members of the band).

10   Mr Woodhead made a vote of thanks to the chairman.
                                    This concluded the business.

The beginners' class was bulging at the seams, so that when genuine beginners came in their first honks and gasps held back the more experienced; so, as can be seen from the minutes, we formed a junior band, which was rapidly confirmed as the 'B' Band. I, and

The first 'B' band concert at Droylesden Catholic club

some others have always contended that the 'B' Band ought to have a separate identity, and not be regarded as a reservoir of talent for the 'A' Band, but it's an ideal that reality resolutely dodges. As with the sturdy chauvinism expressed in minute 9 ('ie No more female members of the band') band politics serve the day, not Mosaic principles. There are four women and girls in the band at the time of writing, and a much higher proportion in the 'B' Band; the sex-test has never been given ... if there's a place, it's offered to the best player. And we can choose from over sixty players.

Derek Broadbent had been restive with us for some time, as he felt that he was having to start from scratch every time a new piece was got out of the library. I won't guess at George's feelings, certain it is he never went into the band room when Derek was conducting. I suppose it was simply a difference of character. Anyway, the result was that just before the 1972 AGM Derek said that unless the band had prepared a piece beforehand, he was wasting our money coming over. At the meeting I exercised my capacity as wayside philosopher to say that I didn't think it was for Derek to tell us

The present 'B' band at practice

band policy; and my point of view was (for once) adopted. We appointed instead Peter Weston. Peter is a pianist, and head of music at Grange School in Oldham. He is a religious man, of a serious turn of mind, though not above the odd dry one: as the band was tearing vigorous shreds off the Messiah he remarked that although he knew the Almighty had many qualities, he didn't think deafness was among them.

At first glance, Peter ought to have been wrong for the band: his connection with the brass band world up to then was largely some compositions he'd done for Carlton Main & Frickley Colliery Band where he played in the junior band. He knew very little about the instruments (for example, he had to ask the range of some of the more esoteric ones). He's also a schoolmaster, and just occasionally the habits of the schoolroom will spill over into the band room: I don't recollect hearing any other conductor shout at a band ('You're playing like a lot of old washerwomen!'). When Derek Broadbent was driven to a paroxysm of frustrated rage and broke his baton into sad shreds, an awestruck player picked up the bits and returned them. All Derek said was 'No thanks, I'm trying to give them up.'

However, Peter has, and had, several important qualities that made him dead right for what we needed: in spite of a sprinkling of veterans (Ian Gibson solo cornet, Douggie Bourne on soprano, David Ibbotson, trombone) we were largely still learning; so was Peter and he had intelligence and the sympathy to want to find out. Also he is a formally trained musician, vital at this point. How much and how rapidly he learned from us was to show later; how much he taught us shows in the cups and trophies on the band club's shelves.

In the minutes of 29 Feb 1972, item 5 proposed that 'Mr Weston and Mr Gibson be offered £70 each [later amended to £80], PA for there services as Conductor and 'B' band conductor respectively. Mr Weston [to] receive the night school salary from the West Riding. This was passed'. This 'night-school salary' is evidence of the beginnings of some help from the local and education authorities. Having once had the misfortune to serve on an advisory panel for an arts association I marvel at the eccentric and lavish demands made upon public money; and yet the brass band movement, which provides a gateway into music for thousands upon thousands, has never had any real call on the money. The North-West Arts Association even has a rule which disbars them

The band in 1972

from giving money 'for the continuing expenses of brass bands'.

By running our beginners' class under the aegis of the Further Education Authority, we are able to make the conductor's and the musical director's salary look respectable, if hardly impressive.

We also get a small grant, which is shared among the various bands. This came about owing to a thoroughly enjoyable public row. The first rumblings were when the board of governors of Saddleworth Secondary school, who have one of the best public halls of the area in their gift, gave a visiting foreign folk-art ensemble a special low rate, on the grounds that they were 'cultural'. The next application before the board was from Dobcross Band, asking for the same concession on the hire-charge of the hall. Certainly not, was the response, you can't claim that Dobcross Band is cultural. At which, Alice Wright, one of the governors, sat up and roundly told them what was cultural. Dobcross got the concession.

Later in the same year, a successful Saddleworth Arts Festival was put on, with excellent contributions from John Ogden, the Pro Arte Ensemble, exhibitions of local paintings, the Barrow Poets and such. A councillor remarked publicly and unguardedly: 'Thank God we got through without fish and chips, brass bands and beer.' This was OK Coral stuff, and heartily welcomed by the editor of the *Oldham Chronicle* who loves a local controversy.

Writing in the *Chronicle* about the proposed grant of £1,000 to the next festival, George Gibson noted:

... I support the idea of a festival week wholeheartedly. It is well run, and it involves a lot of hard work by Mr. Tanner [Chairman of the Festival Committee] and his helpers. But the last festival cost almost £6,000 to run; the artists' fees alone were almost £2,400. And Mr. Tanner says they have increased by 50-100%, so he asks the Council this time to guarantee up to £2,500.

Last year a local brass band (made up of ratepayers by the way) asked the Council for a small loan or grant to purchase a set of cheap instruments that were for sale at Tintwistle, the idea being to form a junior band for which there is a great demand among the young people of Saddleworth. But the request was refused on the ground that the band made no contribution to the arts, culture or education of the district. Maybe if it had held wine and cheese evenings instead of potato pie suppers the loan would have been sanctioned ...

The letters slanged back and forth, but the denouement was in the council chamber in Uppermill, when Councillor Robin Cooke proposed that a grant of £200 be made to the brass bands of Saddleworth, and after the row, it was hardly possible to oppose it. Robin is a sharp controversialist himself, often sounding more aggressive than he means (mind, sometimes he means it too). The grant was passed, but when the next item came up ... the annual grant to the Male Voice Choir (a much more socially acceptable institution at the time) Robin was heard to grind out: '*Now* we'll see the hands go up.' Councillors, not sure what kind of fire they might bring down on their heads, very nearly didn't vote the MVC grant, which was far from Robin's intention. Of course £200 wouldn't buy a euphonium, but it did buy acceptance; now Lord Rhodes (Lord Lieutenant of Lancashire) is our patron, mayors, chairmen of councils, councillors are regular visitors to Sunday concerts, Richard Wainright MP gave out the results of the 1974 Whit Friday Contest, and a Massed Bands Concert is a feature of the Saddleworth Festival.

Probably the best person to wind up the 'story so far' is Peter Weston, speaking at the AGM, 10 February 1974. He spoke with the proper dignity of office, but not as 'I' to 'you' ... rather of 'we' and 'us': as a bandsman among bandsmen. He made the point that as we improved in standard, tempting offers would come from other bands to join them:

'Think about it very carefully. Nobody can stop you, but just consider the atmosphere we've got here, the friendliness, and the village support, and the club's support. Think how much you can lose, besides what you could gain.'

Echoing the words of Les Sutton: 'You don't realise what you've got here.'

My coda sings of Whit Friday, our own special and unique festival. Its origins are beyond the mists of time for me, but its endurance seems to come from the fact that here on the Pennine Hills,

Still winning – in the Tydesley Contest 1974 the band achieved the 'Grand Slam': Best Band, Dobcross; Best Conductor, Peter Weston; Best Cornet, Ian Gibson; Best Horn, Ann Butterworth; Best Euphonium, Peter Jubb; Best Trombone, David Ibbotson; Best Bass Section, Allan Schofield, Duggie Bourne, Ted Tweedy and Ian McKaigg; Best Secretary, Geoff Holt

The trophies currently in the possession of the Dobcross Band: back
row, J. Peacock Trophy, Parry Cup, Hartley Challenge Shield; third row,
Saddleworth Cup, Lewis Vaughn Memorial Trophy; second row, Leeds and
Chadderton Trophy, Gartside Trophy, Hirst Memorial Trophy; front row, Belle
Vue Golden Jubilee Cup, Beevers Trophy, Mossley Carnival Cup

spring rarely coincides with Easter, traditional Christian spring festival. The trees are hardly in leaf, let alone blossom, and the heather has no purple. But by Whitsuntide the valley has begun to put on its bright new green, the house-martins are back, the larks are up, and the lapwings are whirling reckless with love over Lark Hill.

Our day is the Friday after Whitsun, and before Trinity Sunday; originally it was the 'Scholars' Walk', meaning the sunday school children, but since education was entirely in the hands of the Church of England, that meant all the children. The girls would have new white dresses, and the boys at least a new pair of trousers; and they would then present themselves with modest pride and covert greed to neighbours, friends and relatives, to be given a penny for their new clothes. Afterwards they would walk in procession, following the church officers and the vicar, the cross and the banner, and the band, on a tour round the village.

Nowadays it's more broadly based and this is because of that split back in 1952, and because of the work of Alvey Whitehead (organist at the Congregational church). Late in 1967, they, together with Stanley Hall (manager of the Uppermill Co-op), Billy Platt (band committeeman and Noble Grand of the Oddfellows), and Councillor John Bacon (manager of the Dobcross Co-op, a sturdy and wildly partisan man for any cause he embraces–going to a football match with him can be an alarming experience), called a public meeting. General talk was the old custom of Whit Friday was played-out, and that the churches were in favour of moving the event to Whitsunday; the meeting showed that talk might be that way, but feeling wasn't. It was proposed, and carried, that Church, Chapel and Band join together: we would have a 'Dobcross United Whit Friday Effort'. I hope it's apparent that this was more than merely propping up a bit of folklore: it meant that the village at last came together again as a unit; Whit Friday was the focus, but the handsome thing was that it now came to represent our pride and satisfaction that we live here.

Since then, with a growing momentum, social events (whist drives, singalongs, concerts) and money-raising schemes (a yearly draw, and a house-to-house collection ... as much a publicity operation as a money-maker, we knock on every door in the parish) have built up a massive response. The problem nowadays is traffic-

Whit Friday in 1905

and people-jams: where one copper could accompany a walk, nowadays there are two or three sorting out the cheerful messes we get into and create.

Nine o'clock in the morning we begin to emerge onto the village streets, testing the weather with hopeful suspicion, straightening ties self-importantly or adjusting unfamiliar hats, praying there'll be enough posies, and enough strong men to carry the banners. The band is forming up outside the club, George Gibson greeting friends as if he invented Whit Friday personally, trombones at the front ('kid-shifters'), then basses, then the smaller instruments, and drums at the back, polythene bags in case rain curses the day.

The Congregational are sorting themselves out up Sandy Lane, the Anglicans unfurling their banner and leaning it against the wall of the 'Top House', the square filling with old, young, and prams.

Something like this is happening simultaneously in Delph, Diggle, Uppermill and Greenfield; some churches will have hired outside bands, but Delph and Boarshurst (Greenfield) will be turning out. And the march they will all be playing to start the day is

The band marching down Woods Lane, Whit Friday 1971

'Hail Smiling Morn'. Merely say the title over to yourself, and its rhythm can give you the cocky and genial sound of Whit Friday; it's not one of your blaring, pompous military marches: more like the sort of music to please a medieval baron's followers, motley and not much concerned to keep martial step and order, just a cheerful sound to walk along to.

First a sing in the square ... the old hymns like 'Lloyd', 'Diadem' preferred, or perhaps some of the many locally composed. Then the crowd shuffles and turns, the cross, the banners are hoisted, the choir forms up neatly, the children less neatly, and the rest of us how we please, behind the band, to walk down Woods Lane, along the bottom road to Uppermill. More people join, some just follow along the footpath, everybody chatting and greeting friends.

Competition is never far from a Yorkshireman's spirit, and there's a pleasure in seeing how many old friends you can greet, plus a subtle 'we'll show 'em' as the walk turns under the massive soaring masonry of Saddleworth Arches (the railway viaduct) and streams along to Uppermill to meet the other walks for a joint sing in the Playing Field. You might have been on the pavement along Dobcross New Road, but you're likely to be in the procession now; 'Hail Smiling Morn' in Platt Lane, 'The Standard of St George' or another thunderous and defiant march in Uppermill High Street. And on the fringes of the processions and groups of spectators are demonic flying patrols of the inkier village lads, pursuing wars of attrition with peashooters. Bandsmen seem to be exempt, possibly because they tend to have large and heavier hands, possibly because they know your father, but I once held up my hand as a target for one miniscule villain, at ten paces: I wished I hadn't.

Then back in procession, jamming the main road traffic even more thoroughly as all the churches walk together as far as Saddleworth Arches; leaving Dobcross then to complete their circuit of the village, returning by Sugar Lane and along to the club where a snack and several gallons of free pop are waiting for the children. I say 'their circuit' because by this time I've most likely disappeared into *The Hare and Hounds* (pronounced *Ha*ren Hounds).

The afternoon is given over entirely to the children here. In Uppermill there's a cricket derby between Uppermill Cricket Club and Delph and Dobcross Cricket Club. This match is not noted for grace and skill. Delph and Dobcross were once all out for eleven, possibly due to the competitive greeting of old friends, but like foot-

ball and bowls in the valley, cricket is always played with Pennine ferocity and a great deal of shouting. Come to think of it, bridge can be on the noisy side in Saddleworth.

In Dobcross it's the children's sports, and the end of mothers' attempts to keep your shoes clean. If it rains, they go in the chapel and break eardrums; if it's sunny, *The Woolpack* playing fields, for sack-races, egg and spoon races, three-legged races, races for the under-fives, fives-to-elevens, the under-sixteens, parents blundering along risking heart-attacks, young mothers elbowing like trained harriers, and the bandsmen have their own daft race in which they have to play their instruments and it's more or less obligatory to cheat. And of course, everybody gets a prize.

It would be hard to say which is the best part of the day, but the evening's not half bad. The band contest; well, contests really I suppose … there are eight others besides ours. All the bands that have been parading enter, and up to thirty others will come in for the evening. Each contest has its rosetted stewards, its judge hidden and unable to see which band is playing (justice is blind … deaf too it has been said, though not in Dobcross), and a marked-off area where the bands play, one after another. They're 'Quickstep' contests, which means they must play a published march.

Almost every band has a coach, and cunning runners who go ahead (by car) to find out if there are bands waiting, or if they'll be able to play right away. They can of course get the band into a rare mess as well, like leaving them with five minutes to fit in the last contest and it's three traffic-snarled villages away.

Ours is the newest contest, it was started by the Joint Effort in 1968. I'm the Secretary and I had some harsh lessons to learn. I took half an hour off one year to see how others ran theirs; I went to Delph, and can only suppose it's run by smoke signals, because there was no detectable sign of organisation, but the bands played sure enough. And they get in no more tangles than we do.

We advertise the contest in the *British Mouthpiece*, and circularise bands that are likely to come. Some registrations will have been made beforehand, but most pay their 25p on the night. Registration fee is kept low, and prizes as high as we can manage because it's a big outdoor spectacle, and we want as many bands as possible. The second year we were in business, a young lad of sixteen, who was keeping contact between me at the club and the contest

The procession returns

area in church fields, came racing up to me and then stood gaping and gasping, unable to deliver his message. After a minute or so of this Paul Revere performance he managed to find enough air to gurgle out:

'Eric says don't send the bands down so fast, the judge can't get his notes done.'

All the bands, especially the big bands, Hammonds Sauce, Dyke, Brighouse, Yorkshire Imps, Wingates want to get as many firsts as possible; and in any case it's a matter of pride to do them all. So the pressure on the contest stewards is appalling. The bandsmen love the challenge, the excitement, and the charm of the old villages, and I suspect they also quite like making monkeys of the stewards.

A runner dashes in to my desk at the club, reports his band present, looking me full in the eye as a belted earl might regard his own gamekeeper who accuses him of poaching. I note the band down in my book, and give it an order of playing. Then, if there's no band waiting or playing, I chalk the band's name on a small blackboard, together with its number: this is carried by George Brierly in front of the band, so that the spectators know who it is and the judge doesn't. George then walks up to the lane to lead the band, only to find that there's no sign of them ... the runner, as like as not, has left them at Delph or Uppermill just finishing. In the meantime, another band is arriving ready to play. Back comes George, offers me some expletives, and we chalk the other band, regarding the runner somewhat old-fashioned. George goes back to lead the second band; meanwhile the runner's band has arrived and is forming up ready. Ructions.

We achieved a triple-decker in 1974, which led to the following brief correspondence:

OLDHAM METROPOLITAN BRASS BAND ASSOCIATION
Dear Mr. Livings,

At the meeting held by the Oldham Brass Band Association on Tuesday 9th July, 1974 a complaint was received from a member of the Association with regard to a band booking in. It is understood that Oldham Band was booked in before Brighouse and Rastrick Band, but Brighouse was allowed to go first. In a contest of this manner all bands are equal and Brighouse and Rastrick should not have been allowed to proceed to the stand before Oldham.

I would like to make arrangements to attend a meeting of the

Contest Committee along with the complainant. Dealings of this manner will not be tolerated and it is my job to safeguard the member bands.

I look forward to your early reply.

Yours Sincerely,
Michael Woods,
Hon. Secretary
Oldham Brass Band Association

DOBCROSS WHIT FRIDAY UNITED EFFORT
Dear Mr. Wood,

Thank you for your letter of 12th July, in which you tell me that a complaint has been made re. the Contest here, and that Brighouse & Rastrick Band were unfairly allowed to play before Oldham Band.

I have the book in which bookings are made, which you and the complainer may inspect at your convenience.

In our Contest all Bands are equal, and I resent the suggestion that this is not so, made on hearsay evidence.

Oldham band was not booked-in before Brighouse: the order was 21 Brighouse, 22 Dobcross "a", 23 Oldham.

The problem the stewards had, which the complainer interpreted as unfair treatment, was that Brighouse were there, but couldn't get out of the coach. I therefore had to chalk the board for the next Band (Dobcross 'A'), and cross out Brighouse in the book. Then Brighouse managed to get out of their coach and their Acting Sec. asked to be allowed to play as booked; but I had to tell them that Dobcross 'A' was chalked and had the right to play. Then Dobcross, in a gracious and gentlemanly way, agreed to stand down, which I accepted, allowing the original booking to stand. It was a difficult decision at a busy time, but in those circumstances I stand by it.

If you would like to make an appointment to inspect the book, my telephone is ...

In 1972 we disqualified a couple of bands (too many players in one case, setting off without the board carrier in another) but the rain was so vile that we rescinded them: it was heroic of them to turn out at all. One secretary remarked gloomily to us: 'You'll have to play us soon, the euphonium's filling up.'

One small problem that comes with success is the crowds; most spectators are quiet and attentive while the bands are playing, but in the last couple of years there have been a few tourist hoorays in well-cut casuals and tans that don't stop at the neck, clutching wine glasses and nattering while the greatest bands in the world play. I suppose they think it's not there to be listened to.

I make it sound like hard work, which it often is, but the rewards are great. It's as good to see some youngsters in a school band being hurried around in a gaggle of cars by teachers and parents to play some modest march, as it is to see the Brighouse & Rastrick Band marching down in their superb purple uniform and gleaming brass buttons; to hear Dobcross, better every year, warmly cheered by the villagers ('Was band number 22 Dobcross by any chance?' Teddy Gray – judge – asked drily afterwards) and to have the privilege of Black Dyke Mills strolling down playing 'Queensbury' as if the judge could have any doubt who's playing from the first bar of the contest piece.

About 9.30, dusk is closing in, and we switch on the lights in the trees on the little green, the white ropes enclosing it are beginning to sag that bit from the kids swinging on them, the stakes just a little out of flunter. Faces looking out of the little mullioned windows, people clutching pint pots because the club, The 'Top House' and *The Woolpack* can hardly sell you a drink unless you've got a glass, the instruments sparkling in the lights, the uniforms glowing: it's a sight to be seen, a sound to be heard.

The band in January 1975

The 'B' band in January 1975

ACKNOWLEDGEMENTS

I should like to thank all the people who have helped to write this book, for the loan of precious family photographs and mementoes and for digging into their prodigious memories, especially Fraser Platt, Fred Holden, Mrs Schofield Cullen, Mrs Albert Williams, Mrs Thomas, Harold Buckley, Ernest Battersby, Bob Platt and Mrs and George Gibson; the Saddleworth Historical Society for their ready co-operation; Boosey & Hawkes for permission to reproduce the illustration of the cornet; A. Woodhead for his fine photograph, my immediate collaborators Eric Arrandale for being a patient dogsbody, and Bari Sparshott, our tireless percussionist, photographer and draughtsman.